BROTH TO BOWL

To Elliott Charles, Jeannie, Beatrice, Frank and Mira

First published in Great Britain in 2017 by Modern Books
An imprint of Elwin Street Productions Limited
14 Clerkenwell Green
London EC1R 0DP
www.modern-books.com

All photographs by Tom Regester, except page 18

ISBN 978-1-9067-6-191-2

10 9 8 7 6 5 4 3 2 1

Printed in China

DREW SMITH

BROTH TO BOWL

MASTERING THE ART OF GREAT SOUP
FROM SIX SIMPLE BROTHS

Ⓜ

CONTENTS

4
MEAT

5
FISH AND SHELLFISH

6
KOMBU

THE HEART OF THE KITCHEN

Soup is the heart and soul of the kitchen. Menus invite you to think that a soup is a single event, which it is if you are running a restaurant. But at home, probably the last thing you want is 75 bowls of cauliflower cheese soup. What we want is evolution, so one recipe leads logically into the next and so on. Less work. One job = three or four or more, completely different meals, a vegetable tea becomes a chunky vegetable broth becomes a creamy soup. The same liquid can find its way into ragouts, stews, casseroles and all manner of sauces.

You might find your definition of the word soup somewhat stretched in these pages but that is the way of my kitchen. If it goes in the pot, then it has a place. If you are making bone and meat broths, it is a shame to ignore the fact that you have just poached some prime ingredients. So there is a lot here about leftovers, too. In essence, we are transferring flavour and nutrients from one set of ingredients into another, typically water, by the application usually, but not exclusively, of heat and time. Simple.

The first soup recipe that worked for me was from John Tovey, who ran a country house hotel known as Miller Howe on the shores of Lake Windermere and was a great pal and source of inspiration for the food writer Delia Smith. His principle was simple: sweat the onions with whatever vegetable you wanted, cover the base with silver foil and the lid so it was well sealed. He would add a splash of sherry. After 20–50 minutes or so he would pour on the broth, the milk or whatever and that was pretty much it, off to the liquidizer (p47).

I have been lucky enough to study cooking professionally but most of what we have here is designed for cooking at home. Sometimes it is the same thing but very often it is very different in a practical sense.

Each chapter of this recipe book opens with a suggestion for a broth or stock because there is nothing more frustrating than following a recipe to find halfway through that you have not got any. Some people hold that a stock cube will do, but I do not. Broth gives you the base and is the secret. When someone says I had a great French onion soup, what they really mean is I had a great beef broth. If they say I had a wonderful bowl of udon noodles, they mean they had a great bowl of pork or chicken broth with noodles. So we start from scratch and build up layer by layer, which is pretty much how it was done down on the farm. You can build some surprising sequences this way.

My partner's father Elliott is my harshest critic. He has Alzheimer's and in his case any meal is important. In fact, these days pretty much all he cares about is his dinner. If it is not good enough then it is dismissed as 'stuff'. 'Good' translates as OK. 'Pretty good' and a smile and a thumbs-up is very good.

THE HEART OF THE KITCHEN

Also, because he is diabetic I do not use any sugar, which would be the easy road and is a regular crutch for many people but, as we are starting to catch on, not such a good idea. Salt I leave to you. I don't use it. If you want to use it then you can. The same goes for pepper. I find all these kind of additions addictive and repetitive. I prefer the freedom for things to taste of themselves.

COOKING TECHNIQUES

I am also interested in exploring different techniques. It used to be that soup was always thickened with flour and butter and built up around sweated onions, which is fine as far as it goes but very samey – again, great if you run a restaurant, but useless at home where the whole family will respond with a sigh of 'no, not again'. My problem with thickening soup in that way is that having gone to all the effort of using heat to extract the flavour out of the ingredients into the water, why would I want to then dilute the effect by introducing an extra layer of unflavoured thickener? It is the same with cream. A tablespoon is enough to create the effect of a creamed soup without diluting the flavour.

I do quite a lot of what I call chowders at home. It was a trick I adopted to get round the bones-in-fish problem. If you cook in two stages, you can hoik the flesh off the bone when it is cool enough to handle and leave the bones in the bin. This also has the benefit of allowing the flavours to develop over a few extra hours. The same two stages can work for meats too, especially pork and ham. Just because you are making soup does not mean everything has to go all the way. The best meat soups are really ragouts or stews, or in some cases, especially with ham, I will take it out to roast but keep the poaching liquid to use as my broth. As to chicken, well, that is a long story, which starts on page 66. Two-stage cooking also takes out a lot of the stress, too.

Many Asian soups follow this two-stage route and deliver radically different results – see my rich man's pho (p101). It is still soup but literally a world apart, and although some take a fair bit of setting up, in practice they are then ready to go without too much last-minute fuss.

My mum used to make something she called a 'ravasse', not a word I have found in any dictionary. She said it came from the south-west of France. It is a useful technique here for using up meats that have been cooked in the broth, or to give a different approach to a simple broth. Her recipe was 'ravasse stuffing made with breadcrumbs soaked in milk and squeezed dry, mixed with egg yolks, chopped meat, ham, bacon or whatever you have got available. This mixture is then wrapped in cabbage leaves, which have been blanched, put into broth for about 20 minutes. It gives an extra richness.'

Making broth at home brings a different dimension to anyone's cooking. True it requires a little bit of organizing, or re-organizing, but nothing anyone might call difficult. True it can take time, but it is the broth taking the time, not you. And once you have started, there will always be something waiting for you to eat when you get home.

The advantage of making broth is that in practice you are setting up a series of meals in one go. The dishes in this book all serve four as a main course (unless stated otherwise) and the broths lead on to a range of soups. The problem with broth is that while it takes time to make, it does not seem to take very long to be consumed!

Where possible, I have tried to short-circuit the whole approach and combine the making of broth (the first stage) with the making of soup (the second stage). Elsewhere, the soups use base broths, the recipes for which can be found at the start of each chapter.

Broth underpins all other cooking, be it a casserole, a sauce or, of course, a soup. Our canvas is being streaked with colours. We are applying underlying flavours. As in painting, we are creating layers.

SO IS SOUP GOOD FOR YOU?

The answer – as we are using fresh, fundamental ingredients and not dilutions, packets or convenience foods – is yes, the soups here are nutritionally extremely good for you.

The absolute key to any diet is that your body is able to digest the goodness in the foods efficiently. Soup is the most efficient means of delivering maximum vitamins and minerals of a kind that the body can absorb. That is why chicken noodle soup became known as 'Jewish penicillin'.

One of the big arguments about diet is not what you eat but how your body can absorb the benefits that are potentially there. In simmering down bones for broth and then flavouring them with vegetables, we are condensing their essential components – collagen, amino acids, trace minerals – into their most easily digestible, most accessible, format. And as you are making the broth yourself, you can adjust the ingredients to suit your own needs and balance out your diet.

These days the pendulum of evidence is clearly swinging towards a plant-based diet with more occasional meals of fish and meat. And when it is argued that we should have five or seven or ten vegetables a day, then soup is a very, very easy way to deliver.

Whether combined or cooked in parallel, vegetables provide a great vocabulary of nutrition and often it is the least fashionable and the cheapest that are our best nutritional friends – the celery, the swede, the parsnip and even the offcuts especially from onions (skins) and leek (green part), the stalks from broccoli, the cobs on the corn. A little light work can transform them into valuable, digestible nutri-bombs.

It may seem at first glance that we are using humble, cheap everyday ingredients, but for the most part these are what our bodies need and crave. We have become very wasteful as a society. We like our meat to be neat little red fillets. But much, if not most, of the nutritional benefits of eating meat at all are to be found in and around the bones, the marrow, the collagen-rich elements like cheek and trotter. We buy breast of chicken and ignore the rest of the bird, despite knowing through history that a soup made from the carcass has always been given as a restorative. So too was beef tea.

Much of all this was known (instinctively or otherwise) to our mothers and grandmothers. You can wean babies on soup, helping children's neural and physical development. Homemade soup is a missing link not found in fast or processed foods.

The summation of all this is that we are working with the essential elements of what good food can be. It is not a bitter pill to take as a medicine, but the reverse: the optimum form of cooking, proven not just over a few years but millennia. Soup tastes wonderful, which is why it survives.

There have been huge leaps forward in our understanding of how the body takes on its nutrients. What is important and what is not. Granny was right: soup is an optimum form of nutrition. It allows you to bring on board a diversity of vitamins and minerals in an ideal form. It does not matter whether you want to lose weight, run a marathon or just have a good dinner. The principles are essentially the same. It helps, though, to make it yourself. That way you know what you are putting in and getting out. I am happy to say all the recipes in this book are highly likely to make you feel good.

THE HEART OF THE KITCHEN

1
THE BASICS

The great thing about making good soup is that it is usually five minutes hard work to get started, but after that you just have to have faith that the liquids will infuse and do the work for you. You need the right tools – a sharp knife, chopping board and a pot, and that is pretty much it. Many recipes hint that soup is just a way of using up leftovers, but for me that is a mistake. You need the best ingredients you can afford, albeit most of the best soup ingredients – carrot, onion, scrag ends of meat – are not expensive.

Soup is the start of a week's cooking, not an afterthought. It is the first job to get on with after shopping. That way you can set up meals for most of the week. Equally a good broth is a healthy and rewarding alternative to coffee or tea, so it pays to make more rather than less. I have used a standard measure here of four litres, but if you have a bigger pot, or a bigger family or more friends on their way, just double up. Or with meats, extend the cooking time some to get the last ounce of goodness.
It won't go to waste.

GETTING STARTED

All the recipes in this book begin with a good broth, but the words broth and stock are often misused. For me it is a simple distinction. Broth is what we do at home. Stock is what you make for a restaurant.

Broth should not aspire to be the same thing every time. It is a looser approach, jazz if you like, making use of ingredients that are in season and inexpensive. It should be different each time, like the weather is different, like dialects are different: similar but allowing for local accents. It should be able to mingle with other ingredients like a band providing a backing track, or even an orchestra playing behind some other soloist.

Broth by definition is lighter, quicker, a more domestic approach than stock, informed perhaps by the same ideas but essentially and necessarily a pared-back approach, an abstract if you like, even though it shares the same transfer of flavour and nutrition from bones, aromatics into water or wine or other liquid. A good broth should be drinkable as it is. Many recipes for soups and casseroles longingly call for stock but it is really a misnomer. What they mean is broth. A good broth does the job. The language has just not caught up.

Stock recipes are also quite precise, like a medieval code of honour. There should be exactly this amount of this ingredient, the timing should be just so, the reduction should be exactly one third. The ambition was to produce the same flavour anywhere in the world. A demi-glaze should be the same in Paris, in New York, in London.

Much cooking these days focuses on the short and fast, especially in restaurants. The flavours and seasonings are only added at the very end. Think of it like painting a picture. It is a quick sleight of hand. A daub of colour. A cartoon even.

Broths, on the other hand, are slow and calm, although there is not really much work in them. Once set up, a broth pretty much looks after itself until it needs decanting and the base ingredients separated, either to use or to be thrown away. But what you get in return is a liquid with a real depth of flavour that can underpin all your other cooking.

THE SIX BROTHS

The six main broths in this book – vegetable, potassium broth, chicken, beef bone, lobster or prawn and kombu – are the key foundations from which to build a soup repertoire. There are variations given as well, such as techniques for both poached and roast meat broths, as well as bollito misto and oxtail. The recipes work two ways: a basic broth recipe is given and then further recipes incorporate that broth into a diverse range of dishes, but there are also recipes in which you make the broth with the soup as you go. These robust broths transform into mouth-watering soups that will add an abundance of nutritional value and taste to the diet.

BUYING THE INGREDIENTS

I like clean flavours. I like foods that essentially taste of themselves, not some complex gastronomic puzzle. For me, cooking is all about ingredients. You want the best you can find. My dad would go to the butchery department of Harrods. He said that most people shopping there wanted only choice cuts of fillet and sirloin. He would come out with all the other bits – the scrag, the chuck, the blade, the neck – which would still have all the flavour. And he was right.

Some old cookery books say you should use a few vegetable trimmings and any old bones for your broth, but I disagree. Start with good ingredients and they will influence all your cooking. But you have to be alert to local fashions or you might find that your marrowbones cost more than your brisket. Veal bones are always nabbed quickly for restaurant broths.

Where everyone has a weather eye on the cost of a roast, the trade in trotters and tongues can be a bit random. Marrowbones used to go to the dog. These days they can be more expensive than a piece of prime steak. In my local supermarket, ham hocks, cheeks, shins, scrag or neck, ears – which for many decades had been parcelled up for old ladies who knew what to do with them – disappeared for a while when supermarkets industrialized the meat business. When they came back, they were treated like little fancy starlets and priced accordingly. If you are paying more for your bones than your meats, then something is probably wrong.

As the Western diet has become faster and more processed, less and less collagen finds its way into the food chain (much of it diverted ironically to pet food). But collagen is what helps to keep our bodies supple, our nails strong, hair shiny. It helps recovery from sports injuries and directly impacts diseases like arthritis and osteoporosis. It is found in the gristle and cartilage around the bones.

As we get older or if we get ill or maybe just because we do not find collagen in the diet we start to get depleted. Bone broth tops it up. The same argument holds good for amino acids. Glycine stimulates the digestion, Glutamine supports the liver, proteoglycan has been shown to improve libido. The marrow in the bones supports the process of hemotopoesis, which among other things helps move oxygen around the body. All of these components are leached from the bones by slow cooking for bone broth.

For vegetables I buy the best I can find. Soup for me is not using up leftovers. It can be hard enough getting the flavour out of them in the first place without setting the bar even higher by using old soft pliant plants. Some things are worth sourcing anyway for future use like dried mushrooms and pulses. For fish the word is always, always fresh is best.

A NOTE ON QUANTITIES

The practical reality is that the only thing that is going to matter as far as quantities are concerned is the size and shape of your stockpot. Many bones, for obvious reasons, just do not come in neat little shapes. Some do – oxtails and flat or short ribs, for example. Others, like knuckles, are just ungainly. And if you want to go down the road of using the tongue, you probably haven't got a pan that is going to be big enough, unless your butcher is going to slice it up for you. You have to judge these things by eye. The critical thing is simply that the solid ingredients should always be submerged. If they rise above the liquid then the exposed parts can burn and taint the rest. Like a painter, use your eyes, not your scales.

COOK SLOWLY

The extraction or infusion of flavours takes time. There is no point rushing it by trying to turn up the heat. Boiling is not a word I am going to use in this book except where I precisely mean to boil. Simmering is fine. Take it easy. A few light ripples across the surface are fine. No bubbles. Or just tiny ones. You want a steady heat.

Many broth recipes suggest that you have a big pan on the back of the stove and keep it bubbling away for a few days. That is a romantic homely image but for slow cooking I usually prefer the oven. Less mess. Calmer. Steady heat. Out of sight. And usually you can smell when the broth starts to come good.

Cooking on top of the stove tends to create evaporation. It takes up a ring. And there is always something hot and alive in a clean kitchen. So I prefer to use the hob to start things off and to finish them. Cooking on top of the hob is fine for short cooking of a light chicken broth or vegetables or fish but meats need a bit more beating up.

There is, of course, a certain machismo (or perhaps that should be feminismo) to slow cooking, a holy grail of seeking the last nano-nutrient out of the bone and into the broth. To achieve the essence of essence. To leave nothing to waste. But from a culinary point of view such extremes are really only one colour on the palate. Intense, sticky reduced soup or stew can become too dominant, too one-dimensional, which is why the majority of recipes call for just a light chicken or vegetable broth that has character and depth, lightness and fragrance. It is bone broths that need the time and these can be left overnight or longer. I prefer to cook vegetables in short batches because most of what they give is going to happen in the first half an hour.

At home where we want soup, stew, supper, we want hints and suggestions. We want a summer's day. A winter's day. A breeze not a storm, dew not a shower. We want – I want – flavours that represent the world around, not a barnyard of sugar and coagulated fats.

EQUIPMENT

Unless you plan on going into the restaurant business, you don't need pans that are so big you end up making more soup than your fridge and freezer can cope with.

For slow cooking you need a large deep saucepan or cooking pot that is big enough to hold quite a few bones and is taller than it is wide so the heat on the stove is gently applied from the bottom up. For casseroles you need a wider base so things can cook more evenly, one without handles that are going to burn in the oven. Mine holds about 4 litres, or a US gallon, when full to the brim (which it rarely is). You will need two or three small pans to warm and finish off dishes without having to haul the big pans around. A wide frying pan with sides the height of your thumb is useful for braising and rice; what is sometimes called a rondeau. When you are cooking, keep in mind storing your broths and soups. They will keep well for 3 days covered tightly in the refrigerator, or frozen for 3 months. In addition, you will need:

· Oven gloves, good thick ones.

· A kettle with a built-in water filter.

· Sharp knives – one small, one big – mostly for vegetables.

· A chopping board.

· A liquidizer, if you like to purée your soups. A hand-held cheap wand is fine and less washing up than a big deluxe processor or blender.

· A sieve with a fine mesh. If you want to be purist, muslin cloths, too, for a deep and thorough strain. If you need the perfect finish, you can use coffee filters to strain your stock through.

· An L-shaped ladle for tasting and serving.

· A juicer. If you have a proper juicer then you can juice a bunch of parsley or coriander and swirl it on to garnish soups or casseroles at the last minute.

· A blowtorch for scorching and browning bones or cooking onions for a pho, especially if you don't have gas.

· Some bowls, jars or containers to keep the broth in the fridge or freezer. Much is written about the merits of an ice cube tray or two, but that also presumes that you have achieved an intense sticky bone broth that deserves its immortality. It is a good idea but I tend to recycle as I go and a few old soup jars or containers is as far as I usually get.

GARNISHES

Garnish matters to soup, it is a visual overture, a signature, a little extra. It is worth having a few in your repertoire. Soups need something to attract the eye, and a garnish is the curtain opening on a theatre stage. Less is more. Garnishes do not have to go on the top of the soup; they can also work in the bottom of the bowl with the soup poured over. The one law is that they should be complimentary – a harmony or counterpoint, not another tune. There has to be some sort of interplay between the soup and the garnish, otherwise it is a just wet salad! You need a combustion that integrates the flavours. At its most simple, a few shavings of the vegetables you have cooked with, left whole, can work well. These are reliable go-to standbys:

ALMONDS, toasted

BACON, grilled

BEANSPROUTS, for added crunch

BLUE CHEESE, punchy crumb

BREADCRUMBS, toasted and spiced with herbs or pine kernels

CHIVES, cut with scissors or lengths criss-crossed on the surface

CRÈME FRAÎCHE, a touch of sour

CROUTONS, dropped into hot oil to sizzle for two minutes

EGGS, poached (quail eggs work well)

FARRO, or other grains like bulghur

PARSLEY, chopped up with a cleaver or bunched and sliced with a knife

GINGER, a few shavings

GOAT'S CHEESE, in tiny cubes or crumbled

GREMOLATA, grated lemon zest with crushed garlic and parsley

PAPRIKA, for a dash of red and a bit of smoke

PARMESAN, somewhat overused but reliable

PASTA, just a few farfalle or tortelloni

PESTO, as with a pistou but with pine kernels or even crushed hazelnuts

PISTOU, garlic, basil and olive oil

PRAWNS, one or two

RAW HERBS OR HALF A CARROT, juiced for a bit of colour

RICE, cooked and toasted

SAGE, fried briefly like croutons

SAUSAGES, especially chorizo, fried or grilled

SESAME SEEDS, toasted

SPRING ONION, chopped white or green

SPROUTS, sweet little shoots

SUMAC, more colour and romance

TRUFFLE OIL, aromatic luxury

THE BASICS

2
VEGETABLES

Sometimes the very simplest things can transform into useful vegetable broths – the pods from peas, for example, or the cooking water from cauliflower or chickpeas. Usually I prefer vegetable soups made with vegetable broth as opposed to the rather overused chicken broth. It is worth taking the trouble to make the broth in two batches to build up the flavours. I don't like to overcook vegetables anyway because after 20 minutes or so most have maximized their contribution to the liquid. It is far better to make two short batches than one long boil down. You want fragrance, not bitterness.

I enjoy handling vegetables and changing recipes as the seasons change. In summer young carrots hardly need much cooking at all, whereas in winter big, fat stored carrots take more persuading to give up their secrets. Unfashionable vegetables like big football-sized celeriac or parsnips are often cheap but bring a lot of character to a soup. Cauliflower too is a soup-maker's friend. Celery is always a good soup vegetable, but I mean the whole head or half of it usually. Organic is always the best choice – you don't want to be making a consommé of pesticides. If your vegetables are not organic, make sure you wash and peel them first.

VEGETABLE TEA

This is a sequence. It starts out as a light tea, becomes a soup and then transforms itself
again and again. You can drink this first-stage broth as an alternative to tea and coffee.
Once you get the hang of it, vary the spices, vegetables and herbs with the seasons.

3 CARROTS	1 BAY LEAF
2 ONIONS	Bunch of fresh PARSLEY
1 LEEK	SEA SALT to taste
2 POTATOES	OLIVE OIL to serve (optional)
6 BLACK PEPPERCORNS	
	MAKES 4 LITRES

Put 4 litres of water on to boil in a deep
pot or saucepan while you deal with the
vegetables. Peel and trim the carrots
and cut into thirds. Peel and quarter
the onions. Dice the leek. Quarter the
potatoes – you can leave the skin on.
As the water comes to the boil, drop the
vegetables in and add the spices. Trim
the top leaves off the parsley, save for
garnish, and throw the stalks in the mix.
Cover and simmer gently for 30 minutes.

Strain and discard the vegetables, keeping
only the liquid. Warm through, garnish
with a few leaves of parsley and add a
slurp of olive oil if you like. Serve in a mug
or glass or take a thermos to work.

COOK'S TIP: *There's nothing wrong with
the leftover vegetables. You can have them
for dinner, dressed with a little meat broth.
Or take out the potato and carrot, dice
and mix with mayonnaise for a cold salad.*

VEGETABLES

VEGETABLES

CHUNKY VEGETABLE BROTH

This is the second stage on from the vegetable tea. The difference here is that we are making soup. This means that your knife work needs to be neat and precise. However, we are using the same assembly of vegetables as the vegetable tea – with the addition of parsnip or sweet potato. We are not cooking this for as long, to ensure that we keep the nutrients in the vegetables.

2L VEGETABLE TEA (p26)	Bunch of SPRING ONIONS
3 CARROTS	Handful of PEAS, fresh or frozen
2 ONIONS	300G tinned CANNELLINI BEANS
1 LEEK	PARSLEY to garnish
2 POTATOES	
1 PARSNIP or SWEET POTATO	MAKES 2 LITRES

Bring the vegetable tea to a simmer in a large saucepan. Meanwhile, peel the carrots and dice into small cubes. Peel the onion and slice across. Top and tail the leek and slice into thin circles. Peel the potatoes and the parsnip or sweet potato and dice in small cubes. Add everything to the vegetable tea and simmer for 20 minutes.

Now dice the spring onions and add, along with the peas. Rinse the tinned cannellini beans and, when the water runs clear, add them to the pan. Warm for a couple of minutes and serve garnished with parsley leaves.

COOK'S TIP: *Stir in a little pistou (p22) as an extra flourish.*

CREAM OF GREEN VEGETABLES

A simple little trick will transform the second-stage chunky vegetable broth into something that looks and tastes completely different.

1L CHUNKY VEGETABLE
BROTH (p30)
2 handfuls of SPINACH
2 tbsp DOUBLE CREAM

Pinch of dried CHILLI FLAKES
NUTMEG to grate
RYE or SPELT BREAD to serve

SERVES 4

Put the chunky broth in a saucepan on the stove to warm through. As it starts to simmer, lay in the spinach and swirl it around so it is well covered. The moment it starts to wilt – 1 minute maybe, not 2, take it off the heat. In a liquidizer or using a hand-held blender, blitz everything to a purée.

Last of all add the cream – it should not cook – sprinkle on the dried chilli, and grate over the nutmeg. Serve with rye or spelt bread if desired.

VEGETABLES

HOT AND SOUR SOUP

The secrets of a classic hot and sour soup are good quality vinegar, mixing the cornstarch at the last minute, good stock (vegetable or chicken) and of course the dried mushrooms – you will have to go to a Chinese supermarket for these. This is Chinese cooking, so unlike in many Western soup recipes, boiling is allowed. You could also substitute potassium (p40) or chicken broth (pp69–70) for the vegetable tea.

4 dried SHIITAKE MUSHROOMS
6 dried WOOD EAR MUSHROOMS
4L VEGETABLE TEA (p26)
2.5CM piece of GINGER
300G can BAMBOO SHOOTS
150G SILKEN TOFU

SOY SAUCE
2 tbsp SHAOXING RICE WINE
5 tbsp CORNSTARCH
4 tbsp CHINESE RED VINEGAR
CORIANDER LEAVES to garnish
WHITE PEPPER

SERVES 4

Soak the dried shiitake and wood ear mushrooms in boiling water to cover for 15 minutes. Take them out and pick out any woody bits. Trim the rest with scissors. Add the soaking water and the vegetable tea to a large saucepan.

Warm the vegetable tea through. As it comes to the boil, add the mushrooms. Skin and slice the ginger and add. Cut the bamboo into batons and add. Dice the

tofu into cubes and let that all simmer for 5 minutes. Season with the soy and the rice wine.

Mix the cornstarch with a little warm water so that it is pliable and whisk into the mix. Add just a little at a time until it is fully absorbed, and be careful here not to break up the tofu. Finish with the vinegar, and garnish with coriander and a grind or two of white pepper.

ROAST TOMATO SOUP

Tomato soup is surprisingly difficult to get right, partly because everyone knows the canned version so well. There is a case for using chicken broth here (pp69-70), but you could also use the potassium broth (p40). Serve hot or cold.

1KG ripe TOMATOES	600ML VEGETABLE TEA (p26)
4 tbsp OLIVE OIL plus extra for frying	1 tbsp BALSAMIC VINEGAR
Pinch of SUGAR	2 tbsp CREME FRAICHE
1 ONION	EXTRA VIRGIN OLIVE OIL to serve
1 CARROT	
2 stalks CELERY	SERVES 4
2 GARLIC CLOVES	

Preheat the oven to 190°C/Gas mark 5. Slice the tomatoes in half, lay out on a baking tray and cover with a good glug of olive oil and a sprinkle of sugar. Bake for 60 minutes, until they are just about to char.

Meanwhile, skin and dice the onion, carrot, celery and garlic. Shallow fry in olive oil in a wide saucepan for 10 minutes.

Tip in the roasted tomatoes and their juices. Warm up the vegetable tea in a separate saucepan and, as it comes to the boil, add to the vegetables. Let everything simmer for 20 minutes. Take off the heat. Liquidize in a blender or food processor.

To serve, drizzle in the balsamic vinegar, add a dollop of crème fraîche and finish with some more olive oil.

CARROT, RICE AND NEW POTATO SOUP

Grating the carrot makes this a very quick soup to cook and creates a contrast with the diced potato. Both carrots and potatoes are such everyday ingredients that we often overlook how useful they are. Nutritionally speaking, they deliver a raft of essential vitamins and minerals.

2 ONIONS	1L VEGETABLE TEA (p26)
1 tbsp BUTTER	Chopped fresh PARSLEY to garnish
500G CARROTS	
250G NEW POTATOES	SERVES 4
60G RICE	

Dice the onion and sweat in the butter. Grate the carrots, chop the potato into neat cubes and add both to the onions. Mix well with a wooden spoon. Cover and sweat for 15 minutes.

In a separate saucepan, put the rice to cook in approximately 120ml of the vegetable tea. Cook for 15 minutes, then take off the heat and leave to stand for another 10 minutes. Add the remaining vegetable tea to the vegetables and cook over a medium heat for 20 minutes. Then add in the cooked rice and parsley.

COOK'S TIP: *A tablespoon of tomato purée will deepen the colour.*

VEGETABLES

POTASSIUM BROTH

If you had to live on one simple recipe, then this might be a good choice. Keeping the spinach and parsley raw in the mix adds an extra vitality, here giving due respect to Norman Walker who opened the world's first juice bar in California in 1936 with an uncooked version of this recipe.

Potassium balances out the acids in the diet, and the sodiums, much of which comes from packaged convenience foods, so this base works as a balance from a health point of view.

½ head CELERY
4 CARROTS
1 LEEK

1 POTATO
Bunch of fresh PARSLEY

MAKES 4 LITRES

Bring 4 litres of water to the boil while you chop the vegetables. Cut the celery across into small crescents. Peel and dice the carrots. Top and tail the leeks and cut them into circles. Dice the potato, keeping the peel on. Add to a saucepan and cover with the boiling water. Add the stalks from the parsley, reserving the leaf for another recipe. Simmer for 40 minutes. Take off the heat, and strain.

If making the parsnip and mustard soup (p44), leave the vegetables in.

VEGETABLES

VEGETABLES

PARSNIP AND MUSTARD SOUP WITH SESAME SEEDS

The potassium broth will give you a more interesting construction to a classic vegetable soup. Parsnips are naturally sweet, while the bitterness of the mustard and sesame offsets them well. You could use substitute celeriac for the parsnip in this recipe.

4 PARSNIPS
1L POTASSIUM BROTH (p40, with the vegetables left in)
2 tbsp SESAME SEEDS

2 tbsp DOUBLE CREAM
2 tbsp DIJON MUSTARD
Pinch of SUMAC to garnish

SERVES 4

Peel the parsnips and chop small. Bring the potassium broth to a simmer and cook the parsnips until they are soft, for roughly 10 minutes.

In a frying pan, toast the sesame seeds for a couple of minutes so that they colour and release their fragrance. Set aside. Take the soup off the heat.

Liquidize in a food processor or blender. Add the cream and the mustard, then liquidize again. Garnish with the sesame seeds and sumac.

SPINACH AND NUTMEG ESPRESSO

This recipe is so-called because it will froth like an espresso or cappuccino. Spinach has a lot of benefits: it contains as much potassium as kale, while also providing elements of vitamins A and C, calcium and magnesium. Nutmeg has all-purpose herbal properties claimed for it, from curing insomnia to soothing indigestion to general detoxifying effects, so scatter generously.

1L POTASSIUM BROTH (p40, strained)
Handful of SPINACH

Bunch of fresh PARSLEY
NUTMEG to serve

SERVES 4

Warm the potassium broth in a saucepan over a medium heat. Chop the stalks out of the spinach and massage the leaves for a few moments to bring out their flavour and break down their fibres before dropping them into the broth. Leave to cook for 5 minutes, then take off the heat.

Add in the chopped parsley. Liquidize in a food processor or blender. Serve with a good dusting of nutmeg.

COOK'S TIP: *A tablespoon of yoghurt will make the soup more velvety.*

JOHN TOVEY'S CELERIAC AND FENNEL SOUP

John Tovey used to run a hotel called Miller Howe in the Lake District. His was one of the first soups I ever made successfully. His technique works well for most combinations of vegetables. The formula is this: sweat down your vegetables, then add stock and liquidize. Celeriac is surprisingly delicate, so the seasoning needs to be careful. You have to be ruthless with celeriac because there is a lot of skin, but you can make a broth from the peelings and the remaining fennel.

1 ONION	1L POTASSIUM BROTH (p40) or ROAST
1 LEEK	CHICKEN BROTH (p69)
½ FENNEL	3 tbsp DIJON MUSTARD
Knob of BUTTER	2 tbsp CREAM
1 CELERIAC	FENNEL FRONDS to garnish
1 POTATO	
	SERVES 4

Skin and dice the onion, leek and fennel. Place these in a large saucepan with a good knob of butter over a low heat. Let the vegetables sweat quietly while you deal with the celeriac.

Take a large knife and hack through the skin and knobbly bits, so you end up with a square of white flesh, which you can then chop easily into batons. Add these to the onions. Then cut up the potato into small cubes and add them also. Mix well. Cover tightly, even doubling up with aluminium foil to ensure nothing evaporates. Leave to cook for 20 minutes.

Cover the vegetables with boiling water and simmer for 30 minutes more. Then bring the broth to the boil in a separate saucepan. (Alternatively, you can make your own broth from the celeriac peelings and other vegetable trimmings.)

Bring the broth and the vegetable soup together and let them assimilate for five minutes, then liquidize in a blender or food processor. Add the Dijon mustard and cream. Garnish with fennel fronds.

COOK'S TIP: *To posh this up you could drizzle over truffle oil as a flourish. Or, for a more substantial dinner, add a poached egg.*

KALE VICHYSSOISE

A twist on a classic vichyssoise – an improvement even, I might say, as this soup is more multidimensional than the original, which is a duet of leek and potatoes that usually has to be reinforced with chicken broth.

¼ head CELERY	Handful of KALE
2 CARROTS	Bunch of fresh PARSLEY
1 ONION	50ML DOUBLE CREAM
3 LEEKS	OLIVE OIL for frying
2 NEW POTATOES	BREAD CUBES for croutons
1L POTASSIUM BROTH (p40)	
	SERVES 4

Wash, trim and peel the celery, carrots, onion, leeks and potatoes, then put in a saucepan. Cover with the broth and bring to the boil. Simmer for 40 minutes. Take off the heat and leave to stand.

Transfer all the vegetables and about half the liquid into a smaller saucepan, ensuring that you have roughly equal vegetables and liquid. Add the majority of the kale, trimmed, and bring back to a simmer for 4 minutes. Chop the parsley and add, then liquidize in a blender or food processor, then stir in the cream.

In a frying pan, warm some olive oil and fry a few bread cubes to float on top of the soup. Using the same oil, fry off a couple of kale florets so they are crisp too, and use to garnish.

WILD GARLIC, MINT AND COURGETTE SOUP

For a few weeks in spring, announcing the end of winter, we get wild garlic. You could also try this with sorrel, dandelion or, in early summer, with nettles, as the different leaves begin to show. Be careful with the garlic though, as it can be quite strong.

1 small ONION	Bunch of WILD GARLIC
2 tbsp OLIVE OIL	1 tbsp chopped FRESH MINT
1 GARLIC CLOVE	1 tbsp YOGHURT
3 small COURGETTES	
1L POTASSIUM BROTH (p40)	SERVES 4

Peel and dice the onion. Sweat in the olive oil over a medium heat. Peel and crush the garlic clove and add to the oil. As it slowly cooks, slice the courgettes and add to the pan for a couple of minutes to colour. Mix well.

Cover with the broth and cook slowly for a maximum of 10 minutes. Take off the heat and stir in the wild garlic leaves to wilt. Liquidize in a blender or food processor. Add the chopped mint and stir in the yoghurt.

CREAM OF SWEETCORN

This makes a sweetcorn broth that can also be used in place of chicken broth to get a flavour of the US South into dishes or as the basis of vegetarian soups.

2 CORN ON THE COB | Bunch of fresh PARSLEY
1 large TOMATO | 2 tbsp DOUBLE CREAM
4 stalks CELERY |
¼ FENNEL | SERVES 4

Place the corn on the cob in a large saucepan. Roughly chop the other vegetables to manageable sizes and add to the pan. Chop the parsley stalks and add, reserving the leaf for garnish. Cover with 2 litres of boiling water and cook for 5 minutes. Lift out the cobs and leave to drain for a couple of minutes until cool enough to handle. Meanwhile, let the broth continue cooking.

Use a fork to remove the kernels so you have a good pile and return the cobs to the broth. Cook for another 15 minutes. Take off the heat, remove cobs, add in the kernels and liquidize in a blender or food processor. Add the cream, season to taste and garnish with parsley leaves if desired.

COOK'S TIP: *You could add chicken breast here too. Or use any leftover corn to make the Native American succotash, which is just a warming through of diced red onion, sweetcorn, lima beans and tomatoes.*

CAULIFLOWER AND WILD MUSHROOM SOUP

This soup began life as a way of using up the offcuts from a cauliflower cheese. Cauliflower leaves are also useful steamed and served with oyster sauce as a vegetable. The water in which cauliflower cooks can be used for broths; so too the water in which dried mushrooms are constituted. This recipe brings them both together.

Handful of DRIED MUSHROOMS –
SHIITAKE or any WILD
MUSHROOMS, especially MORELS
or CEPS
1 CAULIFLOWER

1 LEEK
2 stalks CELERY
Handful of CORIANDER

SERVES 4

Soak the mushrooms in 1 litre boiling water to reconstitute for about 15 minutes. If they are bigger than a soup spoon, then snip them smaller with scissors.

Put the cauliflower, whole, into a large saucepan and cover with boiling water. Dice the leek and celery neatly and add to the pan. Add the coriander stalks, reserving the leaf. Cover and simmer for 20 minutes until the vegetables are soft. Strain off the broth and reserve a few cauliflower florets, the leek and the celery.

In a separate saucepan add the mushrooms and their soaking liquid. Top up with a cup of the cauliflower broth (the remaining broth can be added to another vegetable broth). Break off the florets from the cauliflower – two per serving. Add in the leek and celery. Warm through and serve each bowl with several leaves of coriander.

PORCINI, FARRO AND CHESTNUT SOUP

A luxurious, recuperative autumn soup, in which the farro and the mushrooms star.
If you have fresh porcini, they can be sliced straight into the pan.

100G DRIED PORCINI	2 CLOVES GARLIC
2 SHALLOTS	75G FARRO
1 tbsp OLIVE OIL	100G cooked CHESTNUTS
4 NEW or SALAD POTATOES	
	SERVES 4

First, soak the dried porcini in boiling water to cover, to reconstitute, for 10–15 minutes. Skin and slice the two shallots and warm through in olive oil in a saucepan. Cut the salad potatoes into small cubes and add to the shallots. Cook gently so as not to catch for 10 minutes. Peel and crush the garlic and add to the pan. Cook for a further 10 minutes, adding more oil if needed.

Cut the mushrooms with scissors into small pieces and add them, along with the water they soaked in, to the pan.

Add the farro and let everything bubble quietly for 15 minutes, adding more water if required. Finally add the chestnuts and warm through.

COOK'S NOTE: *Farro is sometimes called emmer and is the ancient grain that was grown in Italy before the easier-to-hull durum wheat took over. Vacuum-packed cooked chestnuts are one of the twenty-first century's great leaps forward over fresh but if you want the romance of roasting chestnuts over a coal fire I won't stop you.*

SUMMER FARMHOUSE SOUP

This clever little combination makes a great soup. You need the slate-grey lentils from Puy, which hold their shape, rather than the red or green versions which tend to become mushier more quickly. Pulses tend to take longer to cook if they are older, but lentils do not need to be soaked beforehand. For a meaty variation, add thick-cut pieces of bacon. You could use the broth made in the first half of this recipe for other dishes too.

For the broth	For the soup
OLIVE OIL to coat	Knob of BUTTER
2 CLOVES GARLIC	100G ONIONS
1 SHALLOT	100G PURPLE SPROUTING BROCCOLI
1 CARROT	100G young CARROTS
2 stalks CELERY	100G tinned BLACK EYE BEANS
300G of PUY LENTILS	1 large TOMATO
1 tbsp THYME	Bunch of fresh PARSLEY
	SERVES 4

To make the broth, brush a wide saucepan with oil and heat over a medium heat. Peel and dice the garlic and add to the oil. Peel and dice the shallot and slow fry while you trim and dice the carrots and celery; add to the pan. Let everything soften for about 5 minutes, until almost translucent. Then add the lentils and thyme, stir well and cover with 1 litre of water. Simmer for 20 minutes. Strain and keep broth and vegetables separate.

To make the soup, melt the butter in a wide heavy saucepan. Peel and dice the onion and sweat gently while you work through the other vegetables. Chop the broccoli into small stems – small enough to fit on a soup spoon. Halve the carrots and dice. Add in and stir well. Strain and rinse the beans. Add to the mix. Top up with the broth, ensuring everything is covered. Simmer for 15 minutes.

Chop the tomato and add with the reserved cooked vegetables and lentils from the broth, and cook for another 5 minutes. Garnish with parsley leaves.

CHICKPEA SOUP WITH LEEKS, CORIANDER AND TOMATOES

Chickpeas always seem to end up as hummus but this soup shows them
off in another guise. The slow-roast tomatoes provide an edge.

200G dried CHICKPEAS
3 LEEKS
Bunch of CORIANDER

12 small VINE TOMATOES
EXTRA VIRGIN OLIVE OIL to serve

SERVES 4

Soak the dried chickpeas overnight in a couple of litres of water, ensuring that they are well covered. The next day, strain and discard the water.

Pour a fresh litre of water into a pan. Add the chickpeas and bring to the boil. As it is heating, trim the leeks and cut into them into thumb-length chunks. Separate the coriander leaves from the stalks and reserve the leaves. Add the leeks and coriander stalks to the pan. Cook for up to 2 hours over a low heat until soft (this may only take an hour).

Pan fry the tomatoes, or bake them at 180°C/Gas mark 4 for 20 minutes, until they start to lose their shape. Add to the soup. Garnish with chopped coriander and serve with a good glug of olive oil.

COOK'S TIP: *This also works as a salad, if you strain off the liquid. The remaining broth can then be used in other dishes.*

COCONUT SOUP

This dish is delicious as a soup in its own right, but it can also act as a broth for making a curry and it goes well with fish or chicken. Omit the fish sauce to make it vegetarian.

Bunch of fresh CORIANDER
2 stalks LEMONGRASS
3 SHALLOTS
Finger of GINGER or GALANGAL
12 KAFFIR LIME LEAVES
5 MUSHROOMS
4 GARLIC CLOVES
2-4 fresh RED CHILLIES to taste

880ML COCONUT MILK (or combine
440ML COCONUT MILK with
440ML VEGETABLE TEA (p26) or
POACHED CHICKEN BROTH (p70))
2 tbsp PALM SUGAR
3 LIMES, cut into wedges
3 tbsp FISH SAUCE (optional)

SERVES 4

First, get all your ingredients ready. Trim the leaves off the coriander; use the stalks for the broth and reserve the leaves for garnish. Bash the lemongrass stalks until they bruise. Peel and slice the shallots. Peel and pound the ginger. Tear the lime leaves. Slice the mushrooms; add only the stalks to the mix and reserve the tops. Peel and dice the garlic. Eviscerate the chilli and flip out the seeds.

Heat the coconut milk in a saucepan over a low heat and add the ingredients one by one. Stir everything together. Turn up the heat and bring to a simmer and cook covered as slowly as possible for 20 minutes. Then strain and discard all the solids.

To this broth add the sliced mushrooms, the sugar, some fresh squeezed lime juice and the fish sauce if desired. Bring back to a simmer to cook the mushrooms, 2–3 minutes tops, garnish with the coriander leaves, and serve with remaining lime wedges.

COOK'S TIP: *For a more substantial meal, try adding chicken breast, fresh fish, prawns or scallops.*

LAKSA

There are many versions of laksa, so you can feel empowered to use whatever seasonings you have to hand in the store cupboard. Obviously in the old days the paste would have been ground in a pestle and mortar, but a food processor is a lot quicker, if a little less mindful.

2 fresh RED CHILLIES
1 stalk LEMONGRASS
2 cloves GARLIC
1 LIME
Handful of fresh CORIANDER LEAVES
Handful of fresh MINT LEAVES

3 tbsp TURMERIC (powder or freshly grated)
3 tbsp VEGETABLE OIL
400ml COCONUT MILK
Dash of FISH SAUCE (optional)
100G RICE NOODLES

SERVES 4

Put the chillies and lemongrass in a food processor. Peel and add the garlic. Peel the lime and add the segments whole. Add the coriander and mint. Add the turmeric and oil and grind to a paste.

In a wok or saucepan, fry the paste for a minute to release the essential oils, stirring constantly so it does not burn. Add the coconut milk and a few drops of fish sauce and cook for 15 minutes.

Cook the noodles separately in boiling water. Drain over the soup bowls to warm them (emptying any water from the bowls afterwards). Divide the noodles between the bowls and cover with the soup.

COOK'S TIP: *To vary this recipe, add chicken breast, prawns, mussels, scallops or white fish; for a vegetarian version, try adding peanuts, cucumber and beansprouts.*

TWICE-COOKED
SWEET POTATO SOUP

This is a two-stage recipe that makes use all parts of the vegetables. Use the ends of the vegetables for the broth in stage one and keep the choice bits back for the soup in stage two. This is especially good for using up big cheap sweet potatoes.

5 CARROTS	5 small POTATOES
2 SWEET POTATOES	Bunch of fresh PARSLEY
1 ONION	
3 LEEKS	SERVES 4
1 head CELERY	

First, make the broth. Bring 1 litre of water to the boil in a large saucepan. Roughly chop the ends off the carrots. Peel one of the sweet potatoes and slice. Peel, trim and quarter the onion. Top and tail the leeks and celery. Add all peelings and the end cuts only to the water so it is a busy mix. Add the parsley stems, reserving the leaf for garnish. Bring to a simmer, cover and cook for 35 minutes. Drain, discard the vegetables and reserve the liquid.

Now it's time for stage two. Trim the vegetables neatly into small shapes that will fit on a spoon. Split the carrots lengthwise and quarter, then dice. Peel the second sweet potato and dice small like the carrot. Cut the leeks lengthwise then across, and neatly slice the rest of the celery. Add everything to the broth. Peel and dice the potatoes small and add them too. Simmer for 25 minutes. Serve as is.

GAZPACHO

For gazpacho, you have to watch the weather. When the outside temperature rises above 25 °C, the time has come. The splash of vinegar works here like it does in a hot and sour soup. Remember to remove the soup from the freezer 30 minutes or more before you need it. Any little bits of frozen soup that are left will just melt in the heat of the day.

100G slightly stale crusty white BREAD	2 GARLIC CLOVES
1KG very ripe TOMATOES	150ML EXTRA VIRGIN OLIVE OIL
1 RED PEPPER	2 tbsp SHERRY VINEGAR
1 GREEN PEPPER	
1 medium CUCUMBER	SERVES 4

Cover the stale bread in water and set aside to soak for 20 minutes. Get a large bowl and work through the vegetables, adding to the bowl as you go. Halve and quarter the tomatoes. Remove the stalk and pips from the peppers, then dice.

Peel and dice the cucumber. Peel and crush the garlic. Mix all together and add the oil and vinegar. Squeeze out the liquid from the bread and rub the bread into the mix. Liquidize in a blender or food processor and chill in the freezer.

3

CHICKEN AND OTHER BIRDS

Chicken broth and stock can be used as a base for almost any of the recipes in this book, even some of the fish recipes. Chicken broths come in many different shades, from light and fragrant through to silky darker shades of caramel, depending on how long you cook them. The more your bird has had a chance to run around and fend for itself, the more flavour it will have. It is a culinary choice as well as an ecological one.

I am not a fan of buying poultry in pieces. When it comes to soup, you may as well work with the whole bird – it's a lot cheaper anyway. It may seem like extravagance, but it is not really at all. If you do the maths in the supermarket you will notice you pay an awful lot for someone else to chop up your bird, more than the difference between farm-raised free-range and battery. A good chicken in particular can feed a family for two or three days. You can have a roast, any combination of pasta or noodle salads and sandwiches, not to mention the soup from the carcass. And because other game birds also make fine soups, recipes using duck, partidge and pheasant are also included here.

MAKING POULTRY BROTHS

Recipes for both roasted and poached chicken broths are given here, but from a cook's point of view, I am swayed towards poaching over roasting for a good broth. They give different end results of course, but poaching for me is less messy. If you are poaching a whole chicken, there is only a marginal benefit in adding the vegetables at the start, unless you know exactly where you are going with it (see cockaleekie, p83). If you are poaching the chicken for a short time, however, feel free to add the vegetables from the start. Keep in mind that not all elements in a soup need the same length of time to cook. Just because it takes an age to leach the collagen out of the bones does not mean everything else has to be subjected to the same amount of pressure.

As for game birds, they can sometimes work out even cheaper than chicken, especially in winter, and arguably are as good, if not better, in a soup than in a conventional roast, which often dries them out. The only bird I have never really achieved much success with is a turkey (great roast, vapid soup), but that probably underlines the importance of how they are reared.

Although I personally find turkey disappointingly insipid, if you have a goose for Christmas the bones make for a light stock that works perfectly in vegetable soups, and can counterbalance the richness of the festive season. Duck makes for excellent broth, especially for the essential fast Asian noodle soup; the broths don't need to be too strong, so there is no need for long cooking. Pheasant makes for great soup and any game birds work well with a glass of fortified wine – madeira, sherry or port – at the end to big them up.

ROAST CHICKEN BROTH

A roast chicken has a mythical status in our family and many others I suspect, partly because of the 'coming together' it so often represents. Of course, making a broth from the leftovers of a roast dinner is not what you usually get in a restaurant but it works fine.

1 ROAST CHICKEN carcass
1 LEEK
½ head CELERY

1 CARROT
Bunch of fresh PARSLEY

MAKES 4 LITRES

Set the oven to low, about 120°C/Gas mark ½. Pick over the carcass and keep any trimmings for sandwiches or another recipe; add the remains and any leftover bones to a large ovenproof cooking pot. Add 4 litres of cold water to cover and set on the heat. While it is coming to a boil roughly chop the leek, celery and carrot. Reserve the leaves of the parsley for garnish and add the stalks. As the water comes to a tremble, take off the heat and move to the oven.

Cover and leave for 5–6 hours. Remove and allow to infuse while it cools.

Strain, discarding all the bones and vegetables and reserving the liquid. Store in the fridge and lift off the fat before using.

COOK'S TIP: *If you are making a roast dinner, it is logical to make the broth as you go. Add the trimmings and edges of the vegetables – onion, leek, carrot, etc. – to the pot as you work and top up with the water from parboiling the potatoes and vegetables. You could then use this broth instead of cold water in the recipe. Less work, more nutrition!*

POACHED CHICKEN BROTH

This broth uses a whole chicken, so you will be left with meat to use in other recipes. And because you don't want to overcook the meat, you can pull the breast and legs out of the mix after the first stage. For ideas about what to do with your leftover chicken from this recipe, see laksa (p62), quick tom yum (p81) or the cockaleekie (p83).

Small WHOLE CHICKEN	200G MUSHROOMS
3 LEEKS	
2 CARROTS	MAKES 4 LITRES

Take the string off the chicken to free up its legs and lay in a large casserole or cooking pot. Cover with 4 litres of cold water and bring to a simmer. Meanwhile, trim the leeks and slice them diagonally, about a thumb-length each. Trim and skin the carrots if necessary. When the water starts to bubble, pack the leeks, carrots and the mushrooms around the chicken. Cover and cook gently for 45 minutes on the hob.

Take off the heat and leave to stand. When cool enough to handle, lift the chicken out, carve off the breasts and legs and set them aside. If you are making the cockaleekie soup, take out the choice bits of carrots and leek as well so they don't overcook. Keep any juices and put them back in the stock with the rest of the carcass. Simmer for another 50 minutes and you will find the flavour develops 'umami' creaminess. Strain the liquid and refrigerate until required.

COOK'S TIPS: *To achieve a restaurant-style consommé, double up the process by poaching a second chicken in the same broth as you've cooked the first one so you are achieving twice the level of flavour.*

CHICKEN AND OTHER BIRDS

CHICKEN NOODLE SOUP

You will get a deeper flavour if you use the poached chicken stock but there is nothing wrong with a lighter broth from roasted chicken. Either will work for this essential, restorative, parsimonious noodle soup, a catch-all standby to fight off colds and flu. I have added some rice here for an extra dimension.

50G RICE
Knob of BUTTER
1L ROAST or POACHED CHICKEN
BROTH (p69 and p70)

50G FARFALLE or other pasta
Handful of SPINACH

SERVES 4

Cover the base of a small saucepan with the rice. Melt the butter and stir in so all the grains are covered. Cover with the broth. Bring to a simmer and let it cook for 20 minutes.

Cook the pasta separately for 10 minutes, drain and add to the soup. Lastly swirl in the spinach leaves to wilt.

A QUICK GREEN MINESTRONE

This soup does not need any dressing up; it is fresh and light and can be made in as little as 25 minutes.

OLIVE OIL	2L ROAST or POACHED CHICKEN
1 ONION	BROTH (p69 and p70)
1 LEEK	4 tbsp PEAS (frozen are fine)
2 CARROTS	Handful of SPINACH
¼ head CELERY	
1 POTATO	SERVES 4

Cover the base of a wide saucepan with a good glug of olive oil. Peel and dice the onion and leave to soften in the oil for five minutes. Top, tail and slice the leek into circles and add to the pan. Top and tail the carrots, slice vertically and then halve and dice. Mix well into the oil. Cut the celery across in fine shreds and mix in. Cut the potato into small cubes and add. Leave to sweat for another five minutes.

Warm the broth in another pan and then add to the vegetables. Cook for 10 minutes then add the peas and lastly the spinach. Let it cook just long enough for the spinach to wilt. Season and serve.

COOK'S TIP: *If you are cooking ahead of time, then hold the spinach back until the last minute.*

KALE STRACCIATELLA

Stracciare, meaning 'to tear' in Italian, is rather more poetic then the English 'egg drop' soup. Variations date to pre-500 around Rome and Lazio. It is not a difficult trick but you need very good broth for it to work well.

4 KALE LEAVES	2 EGGS
OLIVE OIL	4 tbsp freshly grated PARMESAN
1L ROAST or POACHED CHICKEN	
BROTH (p69 and p70)	SERVES 4

Wash the kale and carve out the hard stems. Slice the leaves into ribbons. Pick them up and massage the leaves in your hands a few times to soften. In a large saucepan, add a few drops of olive oil and stir-fry the kale ribbons for 3 minutes.

Warm the broth in another saucepan and then pour over the leaves. Simmer for 7–8 minutes.

Meanwhile, mix the eggs with the grated parmesan in a bowl. Just before serving, drizzle the egg and cheese mix into the soup slowly and stir to shred it. Serve with an extra glug of virgin olive oil.

COOK'S TIP: *If you like, you can use the leftover broth from the cockaleekie (p83) for this Italian classic.*

CHICKEN AND OTHER BIRDS

CREAM OF CHICKEN AND MUSHROOM

If you want to get that deep silky mushroom essence you need to use dried mushrooms, but gently cooked chestnut or buttons have a fresh charm of their own and only need light cooking. If you know you are going to make this recipe ahead of time, then add some mushrooms to the chicken broth too.

2 knobs of BUTTER
200G CHESTNUT or BUTTON MUSHROOMS
1L ROAST or POACHED CHICKEN BROTH (p69 and p70)

1 tsp DOUBLE CREAM (optional)
CORIANDER to garnish

MAKES 4 LITRES

Melt the butter in a wide frying pan. Slice the mushrooms thinly and sweat in the butter. Put the broth in a saucepan to warm to the side. As the mushrooms start to release their perfume – you can smell the right moment, but it should take 5–6 minutes – take off the heat and decant into the warm broth. Liquidize in a blender or food processor. Add a teaspoon of cream if you like. Garnish with coriander leaves.

COOK'S TIP: *If the mushroom stalks are woody, cut them off and pop them into the chicken broth pot first.*

QUICK TOM YUM

This is quick because you have done all the work making the broth. It is also a brilliant use of cold poached chicken leftovers. Literally, 'tom' means 'boils', while 'yum' or 'yam' translates as 'sour and spicy'. There are endless variations so add or subtract ingredients as you find them. It works equally well with fish instead of chicken.

2L ROAST or POACHED CHICKEN BROTH (p69 and p70)
4 stalks LEMONGRASS
12 KAFFIR LIME LEAVES
1 piece of GINGER
1 long RED CHILLI
2 tbsp FISH SAUCE

2 tbsp PALM SUGAR or LIGHT DEMERARA SUGAR
1 poached CHICKEN BREAST
Handful of CORIANDER
Handful of THAI BASIL or MINT
2 LIME WEDGES to serve

SERVES 4

Place the broth in a large saucepan on the hob over a medium heat. As it is warming, work your way through the other ingredients, adding them as you go – bruise the lemongrass, tear the lime leaves, peel and thinly slice the ginger, and add. Slice the chilli, flip out the seeds and chop across into circles, and add. Season the broth with the fish sauce and sugar.

Once the broth starts to simmer, turn the heat down and leave to infuse for 10 minutes. Slice the chicken breast into crescents and add, to warm through for a few minutes. Chop the herbs and place in the bottom of individual soup plates. Spoon out the chicken from the broth, lay it on the herbs and strain the soup on top. Finish with a good squirt of lime juice and serve with the remaining lime wedges.

VEGETABLE SOUP

Vegetable or chicken stock seem to be options in many recipes but the results are quite different. In a perfect world I am guided by the weather. If it is cold I opt for chicken, if it is hot, then vegetable.

1L ROAST or POACHED CHICKEN BROTH (p69 and p70)	Handful of PURPLE SPROUTING BROCCOLI
1 RED ONION	Bunch of fresh PARSLEY, stalks only
¼ FENNEL	2 tbsp DOUBLE CREAM (optional)
2 CARROTS	
1 POTATO	SERVES 4

Bring the broth to a simmer in a large saucepan while you prepare the vegetables. Peel and dice the onion and cut the fennel, carrots and potato into equal-sized small squares. Cut the purple sprouting broccoli across into short lengths. Add the whole parsley stalks (keep the rubber band on). Simmer for 20 minutes.

Lift out the parsley. Taste and season. Add the cream and liquidize in a blender or food processor.

COCKALEEKIE

This old Scottish recipe brings everything together in one, so you get a beautiful broth as well as a heroic winter soup. You will need a good big pot or casserole. The old yarn says this was the fate of the cock that lost the fight. You may have enough trimmings from the carcass to use in this soup, leaving you with most of the meat for other dishes.

1 whole medium CHICKEN
3 LEEKS
1 CARROT

8 dried PRUNES
Fresh BREAD to serve (optional)

SERVES 4

Lay the chicken in a large cooking pot. Cover with cold water and set over the heat. As it is coming to the boil, trim and cut the leeks into cubes. Peel and trim the carrot into similar size cubes. Then pack in the vegetables with the prunes, cover and leave on a gentle simmer for 25 minutes.

Lift out the chicken. Let it rest a few minutes until cool enough to handle. Carve off the breast and legs. Pick off any spare meat from the carcass with your fingers and set aside. Lift out the prunes, leeks and carrot and set aside. Return the carcass and all the juices to the pot and cook for another 50 minutes.

Return the prunes, leeks and carrots to the pot along with the chicken trimmings to warm through.

Divide the prunes, white chicken meat, leek and carrot between four individual bowls and then pour over the broth. Serve with fresh bread if desired.

DUCK NOODLE SOUP

Although this seems complicated and difficult, like many Asian recipes it is in fact a walk in the park. There is always the temptation to do more to this dish than I feel it needs – garlic, ginger, beansprouts and coriander can be added, but I like it simple. You will need to start this recipe the day before to allow the stock to cool overnight.

1 whole DUCK	SOY or OYSTER SAUCE to taste
200G EGG NOODLES	1 tbsp SESAME or CHILLI OIL
1 PAK CHOY or other greens	
	SERVES 4

Preheat the oven to 180°C/Gas mark 4. Place the duck in a roasting pan with a rack fitted so that it is not sitting on the bottom, and add a cup of water to keep it from sticking. Roast for 2 hours, but check back every 20 minutes or so to drain off any fat. Take out of the oven and leave to rest.

Fill a large cooking pot with water. Carve off the breasts and legs and pop the rest of the carcass into the water. Turn on the heat, bring to a simmer and let it bubble quietly for 90 minutes or so.

Remove from the heat, strain and store in the fridge overnight to let any fats settle.

The next day, skim the fat off the stock, then bring back to a simmer. Add the noodles and the chopped greens for 2 minutes. Carve the duck breast neatly, serve up in individual bowls and pour over the soup. Top with a little soy or oyster sauce to taste, and dress with the sesame or chilli oil.

COOK'S TIP: *If you like, substitute goose for the duck in the recipe.*

ST HUBERT'S SOUP

This is a classic French soup, named after the patron saint of hunters and wild game. His conversion came in the forest when he was confronted by a stag with a crucifix caught in its antlers. Here, you make the broth as you go. Any leftovers can go into a salad. This is a good winter warmer.

1 whole PHEASANT	200G PUY LENTILS
1 ONION	2 tbsp DOUBLE CREAM
1 LEEK	
1 BAY LEAF	SERVES 4
1 THYME STALK	

Preheat the oven to 180°C/Gas mark 4. Place the pheasant on a wire rack in a roasting pan, add a cup of water, and roast for 35 minutes. Remove and leave to cool.

Carve off the breast and legs and transfer the carcass to a cooking pot. Pour over enough cold water to cover and bring back to the boil. Peel and dice the onion. Slice the leek thinly and add both to the pot with the bay and the thyme. Simmer for 15 minutes. Then add the lentils and cook for about 15 minutes until soft.

Turn off the heat and leave to cool. Lift out the carcass, the bay leaf and the thyme stalk. Carve the pheasant meat off the breast and legs, dice, and then add back into the soup. Warm through and add the cream to serve.

COOK'S TIP: *A rich Pyrenees variation on this uses chestnuts – about 40 or so – cooked in the broth in place of the lentils and leaving out the cream.*

ROAST PARTRIDGE SOUP WITH CHESTNUTS

This is a wonderful and surprising autumn dish. The partridge is interchangeable with most small game birds, even perhaps a quail, but every other ingredient, like any good cast, has something to contribute. This is a bit of a backwards soup: you build it up as if making gravy, adding finely diced small vegetables from the get go.

1 PARTRIDGE	100G FARRO
1 CARROT	150G CHESTNUTS, peeled
1 ONION	200G tinned FLAGEOLETS
2 or 3 stalks CELERY	
Knob of BUTTER	SERVES 4
1 glass RED WINE	

Preheat the oven to 190°C/Gas mark 5. Pour boiling water through your partridge and pat dry with kitchen paper. Chop your carrot, onion and celery into small pieces and make a bed of them in the bottom of a roasting pan. Place your bird on top. Cover the base of the roasting pan with a thumb-depth of water. Put a knob of butter inside the bird and roast for 30 minutes.

Lift out the bird and set aside to rest. Pour the remaining contents of the roasting pan into a medium saucepan. Bring to a bubble and add the glass of wine, with an equal amount of water.

Carve off the breasts and legs and add the carcass to the saucepan. Cover and cook hard for 10 minutes. Then add the farro and chestnuts and cook for 15 minutes, until softer but still nutty. Reduce the heat to low.

Rinse the flageolet beans until the water runs clear and add them to the soup along with the partridge breast and wings. Warm through. Drain the broth into a jug to serve on the side. Arrange your ingredients into a neat pile in individual bowls and dress with the soup.

COOK'S TIP: *For an indulgent lunch, return any leftover gravy and ingredients to the pan and add the carcass again, plus any leg bones. Add a knob of butter and cook for another 5 minutes. Dress any leftover meat on toast and drizzle the broth over.*

4
MEAT

There are good holistic reasons to go to the trouble of making meat broths. We have become very wasteful in our cooking, tending to go for choice bits of breast or fillet but a lot of the real nutrition is found closer to, and in, the bones themselves. The upside is bones are cheap, nutritious and you will taste the difference. I have split the bones up here into their own sections – because they do have different aspects – but in practice many recipes here are interchangeable. I have given recipes for both a low-and-slow basic beef bone broth and a roasted version that starts out at a higher temperature. Pork – belly, bacon, gammon and hock – is used as the basis for several soups too. Asian recipes sometimes use lamb bones for broth, but in general it is not the choice of cooks. The one exception is Scotch broth (p116).

The ultimate meat broth, however, is the Italian bollito misto – the legendary big boil. This was a communal village affair in which just about everything spare from the farmyard was brought out. Beef, veal, sausage, chicken, bits of pig and ham all came together. Tradition says a bollito should contain at least five different meats, including cotechino or zampone sausages, and different elements would be fished out of the broth at different times and served. Following in this tradition, a shorthand modern version is included (p118) that fits most people's kitchens. Without having the medieval grandeur of a full bollito it will give you a resoundingly successful base for dishes such as minestrone and ribollita.

MAKING MEAT BROTHS

Meat and bone broths tend to need a little more military organization than other kinds of cooking. If you only have a small kitchen then you need to rein in your ambitions to a few choice small cut recipes like pea and ham soup (p112). If you have the space then the first thing you need is a pan or casserole big enough to cope. Even then you will probably have to shop around for the smaller cuts. Beef bones tend to be pretty big so it is more practical to use smaller cuts like oxtail and short ribs, sometimes called 'Jacob's ladder'. Marrow bones are an overrated luxury from a soup point of view but if you have some then poach or roast for 20 minutes, scoop out the marrow and hold it back for garnish.

This is also where cooking in the oven becomes less intrusive and you can just leave things alone to get on with themselves. Just keep checking every now and then that the liquid is not disappearing on you, and top up as you need and lower the oven temperature. How long should you cook? Well you can play around and have some fun but overnight is enough for me usually, although friends have kept going for 24 and 36 hours.

And just because you are cooking the bones for hours rather than minutes, it does not follow that the meat has to cook for the duration. They can be hoiked out and set off on another path altogether.

BASIC BEEF BONE BROTH

This is an all-purpose, long-cook broth. I do not normally eat any of the meats cooked in the process but if you would like to, then hold back the shin and just give it a couple of hours at the end. Poaching meat in the broth is a good idea too, but it is not really a soup idea. If you want something quicker, see the small kitchen beef and tomato soup (p106).

500G BEEF SHIN	2 CARROTS
500G SHORT RIB	2 ONIONS
500G OXTAIL	3 stalks of CELERY
1 glass RED WINE or VINEGAR	
	MAKES 4 LITRES

Preheat the oven to low – about 120°C/Gas mark ½. Spread the meats and bones across the bottom of a large casserole. Cover with 5 litres cold water and heat on the stove. Bring to a simmer and watch a few minutes for any scum that may rise. Ladle it off if it does. Add the glass of wine or vinegar, which will help to leach out the nutrients from the bones.

Transfer the casserole to the oven and leave for 6–7 hours to cook away, just checking occasionally to see that the water has not disappeared. If it is losing liquid, top up afresh and turn the oven down a notch. When you feel happy with it – you can usually smell what is going on – turn off the oven and leave to cool overnight. You continue for longer, just be wary that the liquid does not disappear on you.

In the morning, take out the bones and meats, decant the liquid and store in the fridge. When it is set into a jelly, scrape off any white fat.

To finish, put the liquid back in a saucepan and bring to a simmer. Roughly chop your vegetables, keeping the skins on, add to the pan and simmer for 60–90 minutes. Then strain and store in the fridge until required.

ROASTED BONE BROTH

The French chemist Louis Camille Maillard recorded way back in 1912 that if meats are roasted at high temperatures, there is a complex reaction when the amino acids and the sugars combine, creating new flavours. The easiest demonstration of this in action is grilling a slice of bacon. You don't get the same effect from poaching because the reaction is diluted. To achieve the Maillard reaction, you follow exactly the same methodology as for a basic beef bone broth (p93), with a few variations.

500G BEEF SHIN	2 CARROTS
500G SHORT RIB	2 ONIONS
500G OXTAIL	3 stalks of CELERY
	MAKES 5-6 LITRES

Preheat the oven to 140-150°C/Gas mark 1-2. Spread the meats and bones across the bottom of a large casserole, then roast the meat in the oven for 45 minutes. Remove the casserole and turn the oven down to 120°C/Gas mark ½. Decant off any fats, cover with cold water and bring to a simmer on the hob.

Then return to the oven for 7 hours. Check regularly to ensure that the water has not disappeared, and top up if necessary. When the time is up, turn off the oven and leave to cool overnight.

In the morning, remove the bones and meats, decant the liquid and put in the fridge. When it is set into a jelly, scrape off any white fat and pour the liquid into a saucepan. Bring to a simmer. Roughly chop your vegetables, keeping the skin on, add to the pan, and cook for 60-90 minutes. Then strain and store in the fridge until required.

MEAT

MEAT

ENGLISH JELLY BEEF TEA

The English garden provides an array of root vegetables which often get overlooked just because they are inexpensive. In fact, they are nutritious and worthy. Swede, celeriac and even sweet potato would also fit in comfortably here. The Victorians advocated beef tea as a restorative for any kind of ill; this is a superior variation.

Knob of BUTTER	Bunch of fresh PARSLEY
1 ONION	1 BAY LEAF
3 stalks of CELERY	1L BASIC BEEF BONE BROTH (p93) or
1 LEEK	ROASTED BONE BROTH (p94)
3 CARROTS	2 tbsp DOUBLE CREAM (optional)
3 PARSNIPS	
1 POTATO	SERVES 4

First, sweat the vegetables. Melt some butter in a wide saucepan over a medium heat. Skin and dice the onion, celery and the leek and allow to soften in the butter. Top and tail the carrots, quarter lengthwise, dice and add to the pan. Peel the parsnips and potato and dice. Leave everything to soften for 10-15 minutes.

Then add the parsley stalks, reserving the leaf for garnish, the bay leaf and the broth to cover well. Cover and simmer for 30 minutes. Remove the herbs. Taste and adjust seasoning. Liquidize in a blender or food processor, with a couple of tablespoons of cream, if desired. Garnish with parsley to serve.

MEAT

OLD-FASHIONED FRENCH ONION SOUP

Although it is known as onion soup, the key to this old Lyons' dish is the quality of the beef broth. In fact, the onions are the least important part of the dish, although it is crucial to get them silky.

750G SWEET ONIONS
Large knob of BUTTER
1 tbsp OLIVE OIL
2 tbsp SUGAR
2L BASIC BEEF BONE BROTH (p93)
or ROASTED BONE BROTH (p94)

150ML WHITE WINE or CIDER
FRENCH BREAD for croutons
Glass of BRANDY (optional)
GRUYÈRE or COMTÉ CHEESE

SERVES 4

Use a wide flat pan for the onions to settle into – you can transfer to a cooking pot after they have cooked and before adding the broth, if necessary. Peel and slice the onions thinly. Melt the butter and olive oil in the pan and, as it comes to a foam, add in the onions. Stir, ensuring the onions are well covered. Cover and fry gently for 15 minutes. When they are caramelized and coloured, add the sugar and stir again.

Cover and cook as gently as possible for another 15 minutes. Bring the broth to the boil and then pour over the onions. Add the wine and simmer for 60 minutes.

Cut the bread into rounds and toast in the oven until they are stiff and brown. Divide the soup into bowls with the brandy, if using, and top with the crouton. Grate the cheese on top and place under a grill to melt and serve.

RICH MAN'S PHO

The origins of pho as a Hanoi street food suggest that the original soup would not have been very sophisticated. This variation is an indication of how far it has come – a swanky luxury hotpot. A supreme broth for Asian noodles should be opaque and intense. I prefer to use the flaming oxtail broth (p117) but the beef broth works fine too.

2 large ONIONS	300G SIRLOIN or RUMP STEAK
1 thumb-length piece of GINGER	4 SPRING ONIONS
2 CINNAMON STICKS	1 CHILLI
2 STAR ANISE	2 LIMES
3 CLOVES	100G BEANSPROUTS
2 tsp CORIANDER SEEDS	Handful of MIXED HERBS –
1½L BASIC BEEF BONE BROTH (p93)	CORIANDER, BASIL and MINT
or ROASTED BONE BROTH (p94)	Handful BANH PHO RICE NOODLES
3 CARROTS	CHILLI SAUCE (optional)
1 tbsp SOY SAUCE	
1 tbsp FISH SAUCE	SERVES 4

Slice the onions, including the skin, into circles and place in a pan or roasting tin so the pieces do not overlap. Peel and slice the ginger and throw on top. Light up a cook's blowtorch and scorch each piece so it blackens. If you are using a gas flame, hold the onion pieces with tongs over the flame one at a time until seared. You want them charred not actually burnt.

Dry-fry the cinnamon, star anise, cloves and coriander seeds in a large saucepan for 1–2 minutes, stirring all the time, until they release their fragrance. Tip in the scorched onions and ginger. Add the broth. Chop the carrots, add in and season with the soy and fish sauce. Bring to a simmer and cook for 30 minutes over a low heat to let the seasonings infuse. Strain.

Meanwhile, put the steak in the freezer for 15 minutes so it is easier to carve thinly. Cut across the grain and aim to slice as thinly as possible. Thinly slice the spring onions and the chilli. Cut the limes into wedges. Rinse and drain the beansprouts and tear the herbs roughly.

Warm the soup bowls. Bring your broth to a simmer and add the noodles. After one minute lift out the noodles and divide among the bowls. Drop the beef slices into the broth, then pour over the noodles. Top with the bean sprouts and mixed herbs. Serve with lime wedges and chillies to taste, and chilli sauce if desired.

CHEAT'S BOILED BEEF AND CARROT SOUP

As long as they are not overcooked, you can use the meat and carrots from the beef broths (p93 and p94) but here I use a prime cut of meat, pan-fried at the last minute, and fresh vegetables. I think of this recipe as an English-Asian fusion of techniques.

1 ½L BASIC BEEF BONE BROTH (p93) or ROASTED BONE BROTH (p94)
Bunch of fresh PARSLEY
12 SHALLOTS
12 young CARROTS

Large knob of BUTTER
RUMP, SIRLOIN or FILLET STEAK, 70G per person

SERVES 4

Bring the broth to a simmer in a large saucepan and add the parsley stalks in a bundle, reserving the leaves. Trim and peel the shallots so they are neat and tidy and add to the broth. Trim the carrots neatly and add to the broth. Cover and simmer for 25 minutes until the carrots are well cooked. Add half the butter.

In a frying pan melt the remaining butter until it froths. Lay in the steak and leave to colour for a minute or so, then flip over to colour the other side. Chop the parsley leaf. Lift out the steak in one piece and roll in the parsley. It should still be very underdone. Slice thinly and flash fry in the pan for 30 seconds, then place into the bottom of the soup plates.

Fish the shallots and carrots from the broth, distribute equally between the plates and cover with the soup.

FAST BEETROOT CONSOMMÉ

Beef and beetroot are natural allies. If you know you are going to do this ahead of time then add a couple of beetroot to the last stage of the basic beef bone broth (p93). I love the contrast here of the slow-cooked broth, which has been cooked for the best part of a day, and the grated beetroot, which has been cooked for just a few minutes.

2L BASIC BEEF BONE BROTH (p93)

1 large BEETROOT

1 tbsp CRÈME FRAÎCHE

SERVES 4

Warm the beef broth in a saucepan. While it is heating, wash the beetroot, keeping the skin on, then grate. Transfer the grated beetroot to the broth. Allow to cook and colour for 5 minutes. Take off the heat and leave to infuse for another 5 minutes. Strain, then warm through and serve with the crème fraîche.

PROPER BORSCHT

Borscht is the Eastern European/Russian 'forefather' recipe. You can use beef broth
(p93 or p94) here but it is not necessary as brisket makes its own stock. Traditionally, brisket
was the basis of English salt beef, French *pot au feu* and American corned beef. Dried and
smoked, it becomes pastrami. It is a cheap cut and there can be plenty of fat and gristle to
trim off. It can also take a lot of cooking. This dish would be served in two courses: soup first,
meat second. You can hold the vegetables back for an hour and serve them with the brisket
as a stew. You need a good-sized piece of brisket to fill your pot.

For the brisket	For the borscht
1KG BRISKET	2 large or 4 small BEETROOT
2 ONIONS	1 POTATO
3 large CARROTS	½ CABBAGE
2 LEEKS	4 tbsp SOUR CREAM
1 large or 2 small BEETROOT	2 tbsp HORSERADISH SAUCE, to serve
1 BAY LEAF	
	SERVES 4

First, make the brisket broth. Place the
brisket in a large cooking pot. Cover with
cold water and place on a medium heat.
As it is starting to simmer, peel and
quarter the onions, roughly chop the
carrots and leeks, quarter the beetroot
and add all to the pot. Add the bay leaf.
Cover, bring to a simmer, then reduce
heat and braise slowly for 2½ hours.

Take off the heat and leave to cool.
Store in the fridge – if the casserole is too
big, decant the liquid separately. When
cold, skim off the fat.

Now make the borscht. Strain the broth,
reserving the meat, and bring back to a
simmer over a medium heat. Wash and
grate in the beetroot and potato. Slice
half a cabbage and add. Mix well.

If you are serving the brisket now,
return to the broth to warm through.
Simmer for 15 minutes. Lift out the brisket
and carve thickly.

Now liquidize the soup, including the
beetroot, potato and cabbage. Mix the
sour cream and horseradish together and
serve with borscht.

SMALL KITCHEN BEEF
AND TOMATO SOUP

This is a good recipe if you are short on space or time. You can substitute chicken for the beef and follow the same technique.

300G trimmed BEEF, CHUCK or
BRAISING STEAK, with no fat
2 tbsp OLIVE OIL
1 ONION
1 CARROT

20G UNSALTED BUTTER
2 fat TOMATOES
1 glass RED WINE
PARSLEY to serve

SERVES 2

Preheat the oven to 180-190°C/Gas mark 4-5. Chop the meat into small cubes. In a wide frying pan, warm enough olive oil to cover the base. As it starts to smoke, add the beef pieces and shallow fry them for 4-5 minutes so they are well coloured. Roughly chop the onion and carrot, then add to the beef and let them colour for a few minutes. Take everything out of the pan and drain off any fat.

Add the butter to a large saucepan and heat until it foams and is just turning brown. Put the beef and vegetables back in and stir well. Cover with a litre of water and let it bubble away until the liquid has almost disappeared.

Meanwhile, put your tomatoes in a roasting pan with a little olive oil or butter and roast for 15-20 minutes until soft.

When your beef soup is reduced by at least half, top up to a litre again and repeat the process, then let it cook down again so that it is almost gone. Finally, add the red wine. The soup should be dark and the meat should be soft. Tip in the tomatoes and garnish with parsley.

MEAT

BEAN AND BARLEY SOUP

Grains and pulses are great nutritionally. Pearl barley has dropped out of fashion and is usually seen in a lemon or orange barley water cordial, but that too points to its medicinal value. It tends to be greedy, soaking up any water nearby, so I cook it separately first.

½ cup PEARL BARLEY
2 tbsp OLIVE OIL plus extra to serve
100G PANCETTA or PORK BELLY
3 cloves GARLIC
1 ONION

2 CARROTS
2 stalks CELERY
400G tinned BUTTER BEANS

SERVES 4

Cover the pearl barley with water in a small saucepan and bring to a simmer. Cook for up to an hour, following the packet instructions.

Meanwhile, in a large heavy saucepan, warm the oil. Cut the pancetta or pork belly into cubes and add to the pan. Peel, crush and dice the garlic and let the oil absorb its flavour. Top and tail the onion, then slice thinly and mix in with the meat. Then chop the carrots and slice the celery and add. Stir. Leave everything to soften for about 15 minutes. (If desired add in any trimmings from the vegetables to the pearl barley pot while it is cooking.)

Drain and rinse the beans and add them to the pan, stir well and cover with 2 litres of water. Cook for 20 minutes. Add the pearl barley, spoonful by spoonful. Serve with a good lashing of virgin olive oil.

COOK'S TIP: *Different grains – buckwheat perhaps – or different beans make for interesting variations to this recipe. For a vegetarian option, you could use mushrooms in place of the pork.*

POTÉE

Potée is attributed to eastern France around the Haute-Marne – it is a sort of broth and soup and stew all in one. It is best made in summer when the vegetables are young and at their peak.

450G piece of BACON
12 small POTATOES
12 small CARROTS
5 small PARSNIPS
6 small ONIONS

900G BROAD BEANS
900G PEAS, fresh or frozen
1 CABBAGE

SERVES 4

Put the bacon in a large saucepan or cooking pot, cover with water and set over a medium heat. Peel, trim and add the root vegetables, starting with the potatoes, then carrots, parsnips and onions. Simmer for 30 minutes.

Pod the broad beans and peas and add to the pot. Simmer for another 10 minutes. Slice the heart of the cabbage and add to the pot. Simmer for a further 5 minutes.

FRESH PEA AND HAM SOUP

The Chinese often cook meat twice like this. The advantage is you get a broth, a roast and a stand-out soup – and, if you're lucky, some great ham sandwiches for the week. Gammon loin is expensive, but there is no waste here; it carves thinly, so it goes quite a long way.

Different kinds of pea taste dramatically different – use the ones you like best, such as petit pois. Frozen and fresh create almost completely different dishes but both work well. The broth you make first gives a wonderful depth of flavour.

450G smoked GAMMON LOIN
½ head CELERY
Bunch of fresh PARSLEY
1 head BROCCOLI
300G FRESH PEAS

3 tbsp FRESH CREAM
Sprig of FRESH MINT

SERVES 10

Unpack the ham and settle it in a large cooking pot. Cover with boiling water and then drain off to remove of any impurities. Now cover again with 5 litres of cold water and bring to a simmer. Cut the celery lengthwise and pack around the ham. Add the parsley stalks and the base stalk of the broccoli, reserving the florets for another dish. Cover and leave to simmer for 40 minutes.

Preheat the oven to 180–190°C/Gas mark 4–5. Lift out the ham and roast it for 30 minutes to serve as a main course.

Meanwhile strain the celery and ham broth, leaving a few bits of vegetable in there too, and add the peas. Simmer for for 5 minutes. Take off the heat. Liquidize in a blender or food processor. Then add the cream and the mint leaves. Serve immediately.

COOK'S TIP: *If reheating the soup, be careful not to overcook it; just bring it up to a simmer rather than letting it boil. The leftover roast ham will go well with new potatoes and the remaining broccoli.*

PORK AND BEAN SOUP

This is a broth within a broth and uses a less fancy cut of ham which you can use in this recipe or the old-fashioned split-pea soup (p114). The best bones for this dish would be from a leg of parma ham, but only rarely will restaurants let those go. A ham hock is cheap, full of flavour and does the job; cheek would be another option. The beans and broth cook together to make a busy soup that originates from the Piedmont.

200G dried BORLOTTI BEANS	2 cloves GARLIC
1 HAM HOCK, unsmoked	Sprig of ROSEMARY
1 ONION	100G MILD ITALIAN SAUSAGE
1 CARROT	200G RISOTTO RICE
2 stalks of CELERY	1 tsp TOMATO PASTE
2 or 3 leaves KALE or CAVOLO NERO	Glass of RED WINE
40G BUTTER	
1 SHALLOT	SERVES 4

Soak the beans overnight in cold water. Rinse well. Place the beans and ham hock in a large saucepan and cover with 4 litres or more of cold water, and bring to a simmer. Peel and quarter the onion, dice the carrot and chop the celery and kale. Add to the pan and simmer for 3 hours.

Remove the hock and, when cool enough to handle, trim off the meat and dice into neat squares. Peel and dice the shallot and garlic and chop the rosemary. Slice the sausage.

In a frying pan, melt the butter and fry the hock squares with the shallot, garlic, rosemary and sausage for 10 minutes. Stir in the rice and mix well. Add the tomato paste. Splash in the red wine and let bubble for a few minutes. Add a cup of the cooking broth and keep stirring. As the rice absorbs the liquid, add another ladleful of broth and keep topping up as the rice soaks up the liquid, just like making a risotto. Cook gently for about 15 minutes.

Cover and leave to rest for 5 minutes. To serve, spoon in the beans and any vegetables from the broth and top up with fresh broth.

COOK'S TIP: *Leave the rosemary as a stalk and remove after it has given its fragrance to the sausages.*

OLD-FASHIONED SPLIT PEA SOUP

This is old-school, peasant country fare. You can imagine digging out dried peas from a sack and pulling the ham hock down from the rafters of an old farmhouse. It is completely different to the fresh pea and ham soup (p112). This one is rib-stickingly nutritious and filling; ideal winter food.

100G dried SPLIT PEAS
1 HAM HOCK, unsmoked
2 tbsp DOUBLE CREAM
VINEGAR, MUSTARD and
OLIVE OIL for vinaigrette

Chopped fresh PARSLEY
BREAD to serve

SERVES 4

Soak the split peas overnight in cold water. Place the ham hock in a cooking pot, cover with water and bring to the boil. Let it bubble for a couple of minutes and skim off any scum that rises. Throw away the water and fill up with fresh water. Bring back to the boil, then leave to simmer on the stove at the lowest temperature for 4–5 hours until the hock has completely collapsed.

Strain the peas and add to a casserole. Cover with enough hock broth and bring to a good rolling boil for 5 minutes. Then turn down and let it simmer for 50 minutes. It is done when the peas start to burst. Turn off the heat. Liquidize thoroughly to a purée. Stir in the cream. Taste and season.

While the soup is cooking, remove the ham hock from the broth and trim the meat away from the fat and bones. Cut into small shards. Mix up a sharp little vinaigrette with vinegar, mustard and olive oil – in that order – to taste. Spoon over the ham shards and toss in chopped fresh parsley.

Serve the soup topped with the ham vinaigrette and fresh bread.

SCOTCH BROTH

This recipe is always attributed to Scotland, although there are similar versions in other Gaelic countries. Make the soup a day ahead as the flavour improves and if you keep it in the fridge you can skim any fat off the surface. If you like, you can take the meat off the bone when you put the pearl barley in, but that is rather polite for an old crofter's dish. Be careful that the barley does not eat all your soup liquid, as you need it to be quite wet.

1KG SCRAG or NECK of LAMB	2 BAY LEAVES
1 MEDIUM ONION	SALT and PEPPER
200G CARROTS	50G PEARL BARLEY
200G SWEDE	Bunch of fresh PARSLEY
200G LEEKS	
200G firm CABBAGE	SERVES 4
200G POTATOES	

Put the lamb in a large cooking pot and cover with about 2½ litres of water. Bring to a simmer and cook for 30 minutes, skimming off the scum that forms.

Preheat the oven to 150°C/Gas mark 2. Chop and dice the onion, carrots, swede, leeks, cabbage and potatoes, and add to the pot along with the bay leaves. Bring back to a simmer and then transfer, covered, to the oven for an hour or until the meat is falling away from the bones. Remove from the oven, take out the meat and set aside.

Add the pearl barley to the broth and simmer on the hob until tender. Return the meat to the broth and serve very hot with lots of chopped parsley.

COOK'S TIP: *You could also use lamb breast, which is cheap but fattier.*

FLAMING OXTAIL BROTH

There are recipes that use wine or beer to cook oxtail, but the art for me is long and slow, so the onions and bones do the trick well enough. You can cheat and use some beef broth, or start from scratch as here. The broth can also work as a base for the rich man's pho (p101). The blowtorch trick is optional.

½ OXTAIL	1 large ONION
1 PIG'S TROTTER	1 CARROT
OLIVE OIL	2 BAY LEAVES
A good slug of BRANDY, plus extra	
for serving	SERVES 10
4 tbsp WINE VINEGAR or glass of WINE	

Preheat the oven to 200–220°C/Gas mark 6–7. Place the oxtail and trotter in a roasting pan with a little olive oil to prevent sticking and roast for 40 minutes so they are singed and visibly starting to smell and run with their juices. Take out of the oven and turn the oven temperature down to low, 80–100°C/ Gas mark ¼.

Pour off the fat and deglaze with a little water. While still in the roasting pan, pour over the brandy or alcohol. Light up the blowtorch and set it all on fire. Keep blasting away for a minute or so to singe the meat, then douse with the wine vinegar or wine.

Transfer the bones and debris into a casserole. Cover with cold water and bring to a simmer. Quarter the onion and carrot and throw in along with the bay leaves. Of all meats, oxtail stands up to extensive slow cooking and is more than edible after half a day. Hold your nerve. Once it is simmering, transfer to the oven and leave for 6 hours or more. You could cool it for 12 hours or overnight.

In the fridge it will have turned to jelly. Break off the meat, discarding the bones, and warm through with a glass of brandy.

COOK'S TIP: *The leftovers also go well with mashed potato.*

A MODERN BOLLITO MISTO

This is a shorthand modern version of bollito misto, the legendary big boil that includes
at least five different meats. It will give you a base broth for the minestrone and ribollita
recipes that follow, but can be eaten as a stew. By all means add (or subtract) other meats
if you like but this will get you started.

1 PIG'S TROTTER	1 head CELERY
1 CHICKEN	3 CARROTS
400G BEEF CHUCK	3 fat ONIONS
1 HAM HOCK	
1 ITALIAN SAUSAGE	SERVES 4

Stack all the meats except the sausage loosely in your biggest cooking pot. Cover with 4 litres of cold water and bring to a simmer. Meanwhile carve up half the celery and quarter 2 onions and rough chop 2 carrots. Throw in the vegetables, cover and leave to simmer gently for 30 minutes. Hoik out the chicken and let it cool a little. Carve off the legs and breasts and set them aside for later. Return the carcass and juices to the pot and cook for another 60 minutes. At this point you can take out the beef and the ham hock if you want to use them for something else.

Cook the rest for another 90 minutes. The sausage will only need about 30 minutes, so that can be added at this point if you want it for dinner, or leave for tomorrow's cooking. Turn off the heat and leave everything to cool down and settle, ideally overnight.

The next day strain off the liquid and leave in the fridge for a few hours. It will turn to jelly and the top will have a layer of white on top which you can discard.

Put 2 litres of the broth back on the heat. Chop the rest of the celery small, peel and dice the onion and trim the carrot and dice. Add to the broth. Drop in the sausage if using now. Simmer another 30 minutes, slowly, covered.

Sort out the cold meats leftover from the day before, allocating a few choice bits from each to the pot for the last few minutes. Remove the sausage, carve it neatly and place in a serving dish with the other cooked meats from the broth. Pour over the broth.

COOK'S TIP: *The jelly can be seasoned with a glass of white wine and tarragon and served with the chicken breast; lentils can be cooked in the broth to make a fine dinner with the sausage; or the meat from the ham hock can be made into a salad with a strong vinaigrette.*

MINESTRONE

After all that work of making the bollito, we can make a fantastic minestrone! The important thing is that this soup is busy. Top up generously with more broth if you need to.

200G dried WHITE BEANS
1 RED ONION
1 clove GARLIC
1 LEEK
3 tbsp OLIVE OIL
2 CARROTS
3 stalks of CELERY
1 POTATO
4L BOLLITO BROTH (p118)

100G PASTA (spaghetti broken up, or any other small pasta; I prefer orzo)
100G PEAS
1 head CAVOLO NERO or other CABBAGE
100G BROAD BEANS
OLIVE OIL
Freshly grated PARMESAN (optional)
PARSLEY and CORIANDER LEAVES

MAKES 4 LITRES

Soak the white beans overnight. The next day, decant the soaking liquid and cover the beans in five times as much cold water. Simmer gently for 60 minutes or more until they are cooked (older beans can take up to 2 hours). If you can find fresh beans in summer so much the better, but they will cook quicker.

Chop and dice the onion, garlic and leek, and sweat gently in the olive oil in another saucepan. Dice the carrots and add to the mix. Then chop the celery, add in and leave to colour. Dice the potato and add.

Now warm up the broth and pour over the vegetables. Add the beans with their cooking water – not too much, about the same as broth. Leave to simmer for 5 minutes. Add the pasta. Give it another 10 minutes, then add the peas, cabbage and broad beans. Cook those for a few more minutes. Drizzle with olive oil and dress with freshly grated parmesan if you like and parsley and coriander leaves to serve.

RIBOLLITA

This builds on the minestrone recipe (p119), adding ingredients to extend the soup for another day. If you need more liquid, use the bollito broth. Add in more cabbage or even pre-cooked rice if you like.

2L MINESTRONE (p119)
1 CIABBATA LOAF, stale if possible
1 tbs TOMATO PASTE

2 medium TOMATOES
PARMESAN to serve (optional)

SERVES 4

Put your minestrone on to simmer. If your bread is fresh then dry it for 5 minutes in the oven. Cut into large croutons and add to the soup. Chop your tomatoes and add. Dilute the tomato paste with a little broth and pour in.

Let it simmer until boiling, then remove from the heat and serve with parmesan, if desired.

COOK'S TIP: *Don't overdo the tomatoes, they are just a seasoning.*

5

FISH AND SHELLFISH

There is only one rule when buying fish. Fresh is best. Brook no compromise. First find your fishmonger, not always easy even in the city. When I first started to cook seriously, I would head off in the car to the coast to find good fish, which often took the best part of a Saturday afternoon. In compiling this book I discovered new ways to cook with fish, with the result that, if I ever had to enter a cookery competition, I would include most of these as my signature dishes. They are not difficult and they do not take very long, just a little bit of organization. Shellfish make the quickest and best broths. Prawns, mussels, oysters, crab and even lobster all make very quick bases for soups, casseroles and chowders. They only need short cooking.

I tend to use alcohol to support the base, which makes these recipes very efficient in soup terms – wine for occasions, cider for everyday. The alcohol cooks off anyway but if you are a strict teetotaller, apple juice works well, diluted perhaps with the same quantity of water because the flavour can be too strong. You can use cream if you like, but again you don't need very much to create an emulsion at the last minute.

The classic aromatics are leek, shallot and onion if you must; parsley, thyme, chives and maybe a bay leaf. Celery, mushroom and fennel are stronger alternatives. As the cooking time is short, the vegetables need to be chopped small. It is usually worthwhile having a few different vegetables in the base to soften and mellow the flavours.

LOBSTER OR PRAWN BROTH

Broth is a very good reason not to discard your shells. In practice, you can get two meals out of just one lobster, but prawns can make an equally mighty meal and are the less expensive option. If you are going to use just leftover shells, then double the quantities below. This works as a soup in its own right but can also serve as a base for the other recipes in this chapter. It freezes well if you make too much.

1 ONION	250G PRAWNS or 1 LOBSTER
1 CARROT	1 LEMON
1 LEEK	750ML WHITE WINE or CIDER
Knob of BUTTER	1 glass SHERRY
Bunch of fresh PARSLEY	2 tbsp DOUBLE CREAM
½ FENNEL	
	MAKES 750ML

Peel and dice the onion, carrot and leek and sweat in the butter in a large cooking pot or saucepan over a medium heat. Add the parsley stalks in a bunch, reserving the leaf for another dish. Dice the fennel and add to the mix.

While this is cooking, lightly crush the prawns to break the shells or split the lobster and break the claws. Squeeze over juice from the lemon.

Once the onion and fennel have softened, add the shellfish and lemon and cook for 2–3 minutes, stirring. Then add the wine or cider. Cover and bring back to a simmer. Cook gently for 15 minutes. Add the glass of sherry halfway through to let the alcohol cook off. Take off the heat and leave to infuse overnight or until cold.

Strain. If the prawns are big enough or you are using lobster, pick out the meat to use in another dish and discard the shells. Warm through and stir in the cream.

COOK'S TIP: *If you don't want to use alcohol, then half apple juice and half water would work well too.*

FISH AND SHELLFISH

FISH CHOWDER

I make quite a few fish chowders or stews. Strictly, these are not chowders because I only use a small amount of cream and don't break crackers into them. Nor are they stews, as they don't require long, slow cooking. They are somewhere in between. The fish change with the season but hake is a good meaty standby. I like something bony in there like gurnard or bream, or sometimes a little piece of smoked fish. It seems expensive at first, but you should get 10 portions out of it. You will need two pans and to cook it in two stages.

450G MEATY WHITE FISH such as HAKE, COD or HADDOCK
450G BONY FISH such as GURNARD or BREAM
225G SMOKED COD or HADDOCK
5 SCALLOPS
225G PRAWNS
2L PRAWN BROTH (p126)
2 LEEKS

500ML CIDER
200ML PASSATA or
400G tinned TOMATOES
50ML DOUBLE CREAM
Fresh DILL to garnish
PAPRIKA to taste (optional)

SERVES 4-6

Place the fish and prawns in a large wide saucepan with the sliced leeks. Cover with the broth and bring to the boil. As soon as it boils, cover and take off the heat. Leave to cool down for at least 20 minutes.

Break up the fish by hand, being careful to pick off any bones (especially from the gurnard or bream), to leave clean skinless fillets. Shell the prawns and add, along with fish and scallops, halved, to the soup with the passata or tomatoes and a generous slurp of double cream. Bring back to a simmer and serve. Garnish with dill. If you want a little more edge, paprika will do the job.

COOK'S TIP: *If you like, you can use mussel broth instead of or as well as prawn (p135).*

JANE GRIGSON'S LOBSTER BISQUE

According to the recipe historian Jane Grigson, there is no better soup than this.
It's expensive, but not difficult. It gets better if you have herb or fish broth to cook with,
but it is not overly critical as the shells release a surprising amount of flavour.

2 CARROTS	750ML LOBSTER or PRAWN BROTH
1 ONION	(p126)
2 CELERY stalks	1 BOUQUET GARNI
Knob of BUTTER	3 tbsp RICE
1 LOBSTER, cooked	125ML DOUBLE CREAM
60ML BRANDY	Bunch of fresh PARSLEY, to garnish
750ML WHITE WINE	
	SERVES 4

Dice the carrots, onion and celery and sweat in the butter for 8–10 minutes until they are softening. Meanwhile, take the meat out of the lobster carcass and claws. Trim into neat medallions and reserve and keep back some offcuts for the soup. Add the shells to the vegetables.

Splash with the brandy and set alight, ensuring the whole dish flames. Douse with the white wine immediately. Let it boil for five minutes to reduce, then lower the heat and add the broth, herbs and rice.

Cook for 15 minutes, until the rice is done. Lift the shells out of the pan and discard.

To make the soup, liquidize the broth in a blender or food processor, then add in any lobster meat offcuts and the cream. Put back on a gentle heat and add the lobster medallions; do not boil, but heat through. Garnish generously with chopped parsley.

COOK'S TIP: *If you have any coral left from the lobster use it as a garnish.*

PRAWN, MONKFISH AND SWEET POTATO STEW

Monkfish is often called fake lobster and this 'lobster imposter' soup plays on the same idea. If you have a lobster carcass or prawn shells to use instead, so much the better.

OLIVE OIL | 1 MONKFISH TAIL
8 large fresh PRAWNS | 1 tbsp DOUBLE CREAM
1 large SWEET POTATO | SALT
1 LEEK | SUMAC or PAPRIKA
1 CARROT |
1.5 litres CIDER or PRAWN | SERVES 4
BROTH (p126) |

In a large saucepan, warm through enough olive oil to generously cover the shell-on prawns, then toss in the prawns. While cooking over a medium heat, peel and dice the sweet potato and stir into the pan. Chop the leek and carrot and add. Deglaze with a little cider so that it bubbles, then cover with the rest of the cider or broth. Place the monkfish on top to steam. Cover and cook for 15 minutes.

Remove from heat and leave to cool. Remove the monkfish from the broth, flake the flesh off the bones and add back into the soup. Break open the prawns over the pan to catch all the juices, returning only the meat to the soup. Pick out some sweet potato pieces from the mix – you want it busy but still liquid. Add a good thick spoonful of double cream, salt, sumac or paprika and warm through.

CULLEN SKINK

Cullen is a town in Moray, Scotland. The 'skink' is curious, as it is, bizarrely, old Scotch for 'shin'. However, this being a coastal town, it is probably just a borrow from another language. The soup is smokier than American chowder and more elemental than French bisque. It is undoubtedly one of Scotland's finer dishes.

500G SMOKED HADDOCK, skin on	1 LEEK
1 BAY LEAF	2 medium POTATOES
2 knobs of BUTTER	Fresh CHIVES or PARSLEY to garnish
1L WHOLE MILK	
1 ONION	SERVES 4

Lay the haddock up in a wide saucepan so it sits neatly on the bottom. Add the bay leaf and butter. Cover with the milk. Turn on the heat and let it quietly come to the boil. It will be almost cooked as it boils. Take off the heat.

In a second saucepan melt some butter. Dice the onion and leeks and sweat in the butter slowly for 10 minutes. Peel and dice the potato – you want it to be the same size as the flakes of haddock – and add. Mix everything together with a wooden spoon, then pour in the milk from the haddock. Bring to a simmer and cook for about 12 minutes, until the potato is ready. Meanwhile, skin and break the haddock into chunks and take out any bones. Return to the pan. Pull out the bay leaf.

To serve use a slotted spoon to make sure each bowl gets a measure of leek, potato and fish and cover with the broth. Garnish with chopped chives or parsley.

COOK'S TIP: *If your haddock has been heavily smoked, you might want to dilute the milk. Equally, if you like cream, a few tablespoons won't go amiss. You don't want salad potatoes for this but proper boilers; stick with Wilja or King Edwards.*

MUSSEL SOUP

This is a very easy recipe and successful at every stage. Do not fret if the mussels are sandy or gritty, as any dirt will handily drizzle down to the bottom of the pan. There are two options for soup here: to serve with mussels in the shell, or to make into a creamy soup.

Knob of BUTTER	Bunch of fresh PARSLEY
1 LEEK	FRESH BREAD, to serve
2 stalks of CELERY	200ML DOUBLE CREAM
1 CARROT	
1KG MUSSELS	MAKES 800ML BROTH
500ML DRY CIDER	SERVES 2

Melt the butter in a saucepan while you trim and dice the leek, celery and lastly the carrot, adding to the pan as you go. Leave to sweat slowly.

Pick over the mussels, rip out any threads left from the rope and discard any broken shells. While the vegetables are softening, add the cider and the parsley stalks, reserving the leaf. Bring to a simmer. Now add the mussels, cover and simmer for 3–4 minutes until the mussels open. Take off the heat and cover with the chopped parsley leaves. Serve as is with fresh bread, use as a broth for the Dalston boullaibaise recipe or make into a creamy soup.

To make into a creamy soup, pick over the mussels when they are cool enough to handle and remove the meat from the shells and return to the soup. Discard the shells. Pour the broth into a new pan, leaving any sediment behind. Then add in the double cream and bring back to a simmer. Serve garnished with chopped parsley leaves.

COOK'S TIP: *Feel free to make more than the amount here, as you can have the mussels as they are, as the soup the next day, or use as a base for the Dalston bouillabaisse (p138).*

For an extra swish, or upgrade if you have leftovers, slice four or five button mushrooms, sweat them in a good knob of butter until they start to wilt, then deglaze the pan with a cup of the soup and return everything to the bigger pan. Garnish with chopped coriander. Lightly braised mushrooms have an uncanny affinity with mussels both in texture and taste.

FISH AND SHELLFISH

DALSTON BOUILLABAISSE

Unless you live in Marseille or Sete you cannot find the kind of small warm-water fish like rascasse and grondin that give bouillabaisse its distinct accent. But other mixes of fish can work for fine soup too. The Ridley Road market in Dalston, London got me started on different approaches with its colourful array of mullets, parrot and declensions of prawns. This needs to be made ahead of time, so it is a leisurely afternoon assembly line. The great thing about this approach is that you don't get any bones.

800ML MUSSEL BROTH (p135)	150G HAKE
150G SMOKED FISH, COD or	1 tbsp DOUBLE CREAM
HADDOCK	Chopped fresh PARSLEY to serve
1 GURNARD	
1 MONKFISH TAIL	SERVES 4

Strain the mussel broth, reserving the mussels. Lay all the fish in a wide saucepan. Cover with the broth and let the liquid come to a slow simmer over a medium heat. Cover and let it cook for a few minutes – not too long, just so the fish changes complexion. Take off the heat.

Pick over the mussels and throw away the shells. Lift out and break the smoked fish into chunks, take the meat off the bones of the gurnard watching out for bones, the do the same with the hake and finally the monkfish tail; you want good solid steaks of fish in there. Add the fish and mussels to the broth.

Bring the pan to a simmer; you don't want to boil it, just warm enough. Stir in the cream and garnish with the chopped parsley leaves.

COOK'S TIP: *If you make more than you need, you can add different fish the next day, such as scallops or even lobster for an upscale variation. Cod, haddock and coley are all contenders. It is a good way of using up offcuts from the fishmonger's slab.*

THAI-STYLE CRAB AND LEMONGRASS SOUP

Crabs produce a much denser, deeper broth than their cousins in the prawn family. A broth neatly sidelines the tricky part of cleaning a crab, and leaves the delicate white meat for salad or sandwiches. Ask the fishmonger to break open the crab for you (you need a strong grip and to check that it is not full of water). This recipe a variation on a chicken with galangal Thai soup.

For the broth	2 SHALLOTS
1 CRAB	1 fresh BIRD'S EYE CHILLI
1L CIDER or WHITE WINE	1 tbsp VEGETABLE OIL
Bunch of fresh PARSLEY, stalks only	250ML COCONUT MILK
	250ML CRAB BROTH (as already made)
For the soup	CRABMEAT (as reserved from the broth)
1 stalk LEMONGRASS	Fresh CORIANDER LEAVES to garnish
2.5CM piece of GINGER	
1 GARLIC CLOVE	SERVES 4

First, make the broth. Using a solid chopping board and a cleaver or wooden rolling pin, break up the crab in sections. Lift out the spongy gills and discard. Crack the claws, take out the white meat and set aside. Snap off the legs, crack the shells and add to the pot. Split the head, chop into four and add to the pot. Lift out any white meat from the shell and set aside.

Put everything else in a large cooking pot and cover with cider. Add the parsley stalks. Bring to a simmer, then cover. Simmer gently for 25 minutes. Take off the heat and leave to infuse overnight. The next day, strain the broth and remove the meat from the carcass. Set both aside.

For the soup, dice the lemongrass if fresh or leave whole and bruise if it is a bit stalky. Peel the ginger but leave whole. Peel and dice the garlic and shallots. Deseed and slice the chilli. Warm the oil in a wok and as it begins to smoke add the garlic and let it season the oil for a few minutes. Add the shallots and give them a couple of minutes, shaking as you go. Then add the chilli, ginger and lemongrass.

Top with the coconut milk and broth and let it simmer for 15 minutes. Add the crabmeat at the last moment and garnish with coriander leaves.

OYSTER SOUP

In some parts of the world oysters are cheap; in others this soup may at first glance seem wildly extravagant, but in practice it goes quite a long way. If you want to make larger quantities you can dilute the wine with water 50:50. Do not be timid. This is one of the greatest of all soups.

For the broth	For the soup
Knob of BUTTER	750ML OYSTER BROTH
1 LEEK	(as already made)
1 CARROT	16 OYSTERS
Bunch of fresh PARSLEY	4 handfuls of SPINACH
750ML WHITE WINE	4 tbsp DOUBLE CREAM
12 OYSTERS	FRESH BREAD to serve
	SERVES 4

Melt the butter in a large saucepan. Top and tail the leek, slice thinly diagonally and add to the pan. Top and tail the carrot, peel if preferred, quarter lengthwise, then dice and add to the leek. Sweat for 5 minutes. Add the parsley as a bundle and pour in the wine. Shuck the oysters and add them, with their juice. Simmer for 10 minutes. Take off the heat and leave to infuse, overnight is best.

For the soup, lift out the bundle of parsley from the broth and discard. Shuck 4 oysters per person. Warm the soup plates. Put the broth on a low heat, and add the fresh oysters. Throw in a handful of spinach per person. About 1 minute later, the moment the spinach wilts, add the cream.

Take off the heat. Stir and ladle into soup bowls. Serve with fresh bread.

6
KOMBU

The recipes in the vegetable chapter would suit any vegan, but the Japanese have a different approach of using kombu or kelp for a basic broth. Although the kelp is harvested in Asia, you can find it easily enough on the beaches of America and Europe, seemingly abandoned. It lends an invisible but not insignificant sense of body to liquid – what is often referred to as 'umami', or the fifth sense of taste.

How much to use depends a little on the age and quality of the kombu and your taste. In the recipe for two mushroom miso soup (p154), I have used a whole sheet to show one extreme. For pescatarians, flakes of bonito or dried tuna are added to the kombu broth to lend a sense of spice, and this is referred to as 'dashi'. The kombu should not be boiled but just warmed through to soften. It can also be cooked with soy and mirin to make a potent relish, usually for rice (in small quantities because it is quite rich) or the liquid used for broth. I have seen it used as garnish for sushi, and it also mixes well with other seaweeds such as nori or wakame.

Kombu is a very ancient food and a potent source of iodine and fibre. Some maintain that the north-west passage from America to Greenland might have been sustained by farming kombu as far back as 12,000BC, the supposition being that it was farmed during the same time period in the Far East.

JAPANESE BONITO BROTH

This is dashi, the basic Japanese cooking broth for all clear soups, which is simply kombu seaweed water infused with dried tuna flakes. The glutamates in the seaweed create the sense of 'umami'. It is most familiar as the basis for miso soup.

1 thumb-length piece of KOMBU

4 tbsp DRIED BONITO FLAKES

MAKES 1 LITRE

Soak the kombu in 1 litre of water and slowly bring to a simmer. The moment it starts to boil, take off the heat and leave to infuse for 10 minutes (or longer). Add the bonito flakes and infuse for another 5 minutes. Strain.

COOK'S TIP: *You can re-use the kombu in other recipes. It can be cooked in a mix of soy and mirin for* tsukudani, *which is usually served cold with rice. Alternatively, combine four parts of dashi to one of soy, one of mirin and one of brown sugar to make a dipping sauce or as a base for noodles.*

KOMBU

MONKFISH WITH GINGER

Dashi works perfectly as a poaching broth for the monkfish. Never boil
the broth here; keep everything just below boiling.

2 SHALLOTS	1 tbsp VEGETABLE OIL
1 CLOVE GARLIC	1L JAPANESE BONITO BROTH (p144)
Bunch of SPRING ONIONS	2 tbsp SOY SAUCE
Thumb-length piece of GINGER	1 LIME
2 SHIITAKE MUSHROOMS	Fresh CORIANDER LEAVES to garnish
½ RED PEPPER	
340G MONKFISH FILLET	SERVES 4

Peel and dice the shallot and garlic. Chop the spring onions. Peel and slice the ginger. Trim the mushrooms and cut the pepper into thin shards. Remove the skin from the monkfish and cube the flesh.

Heat a wok or large sauté pan and moisten with the vegetable oil. Add the shallot, garlic and ginger and stir-fry for 3 minutes until fragrant. Add the Japanese bonito broth, soy sauce and the juice from the lime. Lay the fish fillet pieces in carefully and cover. Let it cook very gently over a low heat. How long you cook it for depends on the thickness of the fish, but you want to be as gentle as possible, so that it cooks as the broth drops in temperature.

Lastly add the red pepper, mushroom and spring onions. Finish with coriander leaves to garnish.

KOMBU

SCAMPI, PEA SHOOTS AND TOFU IN MISO BROTH

This is really easy, but looks elegant. If you cannot find pea shoots then use watercress instead.

1L JAPANESE BONITO BROTH (p144)
or PRAWN BROTH (p126)
1 tbsp YELLOW MISO PASTE
600G SCAMPI

200G SILKEN TOFU
2 handfuls PEA SHOOTS

SERVES 4

First make the miso broth. Warm the broth in a saucepan. Then, in a small bowl, take a little of the broth and mix with the miso paste until it softens and loosens up. Add back into the broth.

Warm the broth without boiling, and add the scampi. Cut the tofu into neat squares and float them on the mix. As the scampi turn pinks, add the pea shoots and serve immediately.

VEGETABLE NOODLE SOUP

Noodles and vegetables are added to the dashi to make a satisfying and substantial soup.

Bunch of SPRING ONIONS	2 Handfuls of SOBA or
Handful of BEANSPROUTS	UDON NOODLES
4-5 slices BAMBOO SHOOT	2 tbsp SOY SAUCE
4 tbsp tinned SWEETCORN	3 tbsp MIRIN
2-3 sheets WAKAME or	2 tbsp SAKE
NORI SEAWEED	
1L JAPANESE BONITO BROTH (p144)	SERVES 4

Trim and slice the spring onion. Pick over the beansprouts and bamboo shoot. Have the sweetcorn and seaweed ready.

Bring the broth to a simmer. Cook the noodles for two minutes then lift out and divide into warmed soup bowls. Add the spring onion, beansprouts, bamboo shoots, sweetcorn and seaweed to warm through. Season with the soy, mirin and sake and pour over the noodles.

MUSHROOM BROTH WITH SOY, CABBAGE AND UDON NOODLES

This recipe is a great illustration of how American volume in cups makes more sense than European grams and kilos. What you need is the same amount of fresh mushrooms to cabbage and half as much dried, but of course dried mushrooms do not weigh as much as cabbage because they are not as dense, so you have to judge by eye, not scales. You could use different noodles but I like the contrast of fresh fat udon with the strips of cabbage.

For the broth	For the soup
½ CUP DRIED MOREL or	1 cup mixed fresh MUSHROOMS
SHIITAKE MUSHROOMS	1 cup shredded CABBAGE
Sheet of KOMBU	100G fresh TOFU
2 CLOVES GARLIC	2 servings of UDON NOODLES
1 ONION	8 SPRING ONIONS
2 tbsp SOYA SAUCE	
2 tbsp MIRIN	SERVES 4

Pour 4 litres of boiling water over the dried mushrooms to reconstitute. Add in the sheet of kombu and leave for 10 minutes, then lift out and set aside for another day.

Trim the vegetables and fresh mushrooms and add the peelings to the broth. Peel and dice the garlic and onion and add to the liquid. Then raise the heat back to almost a boil and let it half simmer for 20 minutes. Strain and add the soy and mirin.

To assemble the soup, warm the broth. Slice the fresh mushrooms and add to the broth with the cabbage. Cube the tofu and drop in.

Boil the noodles in water for 2 minutes or as directed. Warm the soup bowls. Drain the noodles and place in the bowls. Cover with the broth and top with the mushrooms, cabbage, tofu and sliced spring onion.

KOMBU

TWO MUSHROOM MISO SOUP

Basic miso soup is mostly the triumph of the Japanese grocery. The only skill left in a culinary sense is boiling water to rehydrate the wakame and dissolve the paste. It is wonderfully simple. This recipe, Buddhist in inspiration, is a more evolved variation. In Japan the vegetables might be burdock and daikon but Western root vegetables work equally well for the base. What this recipe does demonstrate is the full power of the kombu.

12 DRIED SHITAKE MUSHROOMS	Sheet of KOMBU
1 CARROT	3 tsp MISO PASTE
1 PARSNIP	125G SILKEN TOFU
1 CELERIAC	SOY SAUCE or SESAME OIL
VEGETABLE OIL for frying	Fresh CORIANDER to garnish
125G OYSTER MUSHROOMS	
	SERVES 4

Soak the dried mushrooms in boiled water for 15 minutes, until soft. Wash and peel the carrot, parsnip and celeriac and dice into small cubes. Shallow fry lightly in olive or vegetable oil for 5 minutes.

Tear the oyster mushrooms into small pieces and add to the vegetables, stirring everything together. Cover with boiled water. Add the shitake and the liquid they are soaked in, making about 2 litres in all in the pan. Cover everything with the whole sheet of kombu. Cover the pan and let it simmer quietly for 30 minutes.

Dissolve the miso paste in a twice as much hot water and stir well to get rid of any lumps. Carve the tofu into batons. Take the pan off the heat. Lift out the kombu and add the miso and the tofu. Garnish with coriander leaves, soy sauce or sesame oil.

KOMBU

INDEX

ACKNOWLEDGEMENTS

Thanks to Silvia, Lisa, Elena and the rest of the Elwin Street team, also to Zobia and Erik for testing and preparations, to Tom (I-hate-natural-light) Regester for seeing the vision and making the photographs work so well.